AMERICA'S LAST CALL

DAVID WILKERSON

Wilkerson Trust
PUBLICATIONS

America's Last Call

Copyright © 1998
Wilkerson Trust Publications

Published by Wilkerson Trust Publications
Post Office Box 260
Lindale, Texas 75771

Printed in the United States of America

ISBN 0-9663172-1-1

Contents

 **am one of the Lord's many watchmen. And here is why I cannot hold my peace.**

"Again the word of the Lord came unto me, saying, Son of man, speak to the children of thy people, and say unto them, When I bring the sword upon a land, if the people of the land take a man of their coasts, and set him for their watchman: If when he seeth the sword come upon the land, he blow the trumpet, and warn the people; then whosoever heareth the sound of the trumpet, and taketh not warning; if the sword come, and take him away, his blood shall be upon his own head. He heard the sound of the trumpet, and took not warning; his blood shall be upon him. But he that taketh warning shall deliver his soul. But if the watchman see the sword come, and blow not the trumpet, and the people be not warned; if the sword come, and take any person from among them, he is taken away in his iniquity; but his blood will I require at the watchman's hand."

— Ezekiel 33:1-6

Introduction

In my flesh, I don't want to hear the message in this book. I too enjoy the abounding prosperity of our nation — and I praise God for the flow of sufficient funds that underwrites all of our charitable ministries in New York City. Yet the past decade of ever-increasing prosperity has lulled our nation — including the church — to sleep, and we keep hoping our great American dream will not soon end.

Some readers may throw this book aside in disgust after reading just a chapter or two. They'll dismiss it all as mere doomsday chatter by a disconsolate preacher. Yet, in my heart, I believe that every praying Christian and every thinking American knows intuitively our nation has crossed a line of some kind — that God's patience is near an end, and a day of reckoning has come.

I have purposely kept this book short and, hopefully, to the point. I've had no visions, dreams or special revelations — and I reject outright all prophetic warnings that are not scripturally sound. Likewise, every reader of this book has an obligation to test what I've written here by the word of God. All true believers can know what the Lord is going to do, if they'll but take the time to search the scriptures and discover God's set patterns of judging sinful nations in the past.

There is hope in this book. You will find abundant scriptural truth in every chapter. I urge you to read prayerfully the last two chapters, and rejoice in God's promises of faithfulness to his people in trying times.

America's Last Call

As I write this message (1998) America is enjoying un-precedented prosperity. The stock market is at an all-time high. Unemployment is at a twenty-eight-year low. And most Americans are facing the future with high expectations. A recent article in *USA Today* announced, "America is rolling into the future with an economic confidence unmatched in thirty years." The article said that even though major companies are laying off thousands of workers — corporate giants like Eastman Kodak, RJR Nabisco, Boeing and Hasbro — Americans are still bullish about the future. The Internal Revenue Service reports that today more than 87,000 Americans are millionaires. And Americans soak up more than $200 billion each year in imported luxuries. Of course, there are pockets of poverty — areas of high unemployment, with families barely able to get by — but, as a whole, the nation is riding a wave of prosperity.

As I watch our country accumulating even greater wealth, I have to wonder: How can God keep blessing such a wicked nation? I believe every intelligent Christian has to ask this question: "Why do we prosper when we're on a course to rid society's soul of all thought or memory of God?" Think about it:

• Federal courts are doing everything within their power to outlaw even the mention of God's name in public life. Judges are banning the symbols of faith left and right — crosses, religious plaques, manger scenes, prayer in schools. And now a movement to remove the phrase "In God We Trust" from our coins is gaining popularity.

• We're awash in an ocean of bloodshed, as we continue to allow the murder of millions of unborn children. Doctors are suctioning out the brains of fully developed babies in their third trimester. And nurses who unashamedly assist in abortions march in protest against the killing of whales, minks and rabbits. What arrogant hypocrisy!

• There are more than 100 million TV sets and some 100,000 movie theaters in America today — and most are serving as conduits for pornography! Sadly, few movies today can make money without an R rating. Even Disney movies and other family films have jumped on the bandwagon. Most of their films promote cursing and the occult, even among children. In fact, it has become popular to curse Christ with disdain — mocking him, ridiculing him, dragging his name into the gutters of sensuality and violence.

• Violence in America today has far surpassed that of the days of Noah or Lot. Almost every town, village and city in this country has experienced the shock of senseless murders. As a result, many people have literally locked themselves into their homes, afraid to walk the streets. Most Americans are dumbfounded by all the senseless killings, especially among students. Our schools are now unsafe.

These are just a few signs of our nation's moral decay. Now even the most hardened commentators — liberal writers, ungodly politicians and abrasive talk-show hosts — are crying out, "America has gone mad! Our nation is in a moral shambles. We're racing toward anarchy — beyond all hope!"

In light of all this immorality and enmity toward God, I have to ask the Lord: "Father, why are you blessing this nation? We try to remove you from our society — yet you shower us with goodness. We commit horrible acts of violence, bloodshed and indecency — yet you send us unprecedented prosperity. Why?"

There is one simple reason for this — and God's word makes it very clear: Our nation right now is receiving its final call to repentance, just prior to a great judgment! I believe America stands at the brink of an economic and social collapse.

Now, I say this not because I've had a vision or dream about it. Rather, I have simply studied God's word — and I discern from the scriptures that God is dealing with America in the same way he's dealt with all nations who have forsaken him. Indeed, this is how Daniel realized Jerusalem would be rebuilt and inhabited again by the Jews: he simply studied God's word. While reading Jeremiah 25:12, he saw that a day prophesied seventy years before had arrived: "...I Daniel understood by books the number of the years, whereof the word of the Lord came to Jeremiah the prophet, that he would accomplish seventy years in the desolations of Jerusalem" (Daniel 9:2).

Daniel's prophecies came from this discovery in the scriptures. And, likewise, we also can better understand the Lord's dealings as we study his word. The fact is, God never changes; he will always move according to his eternal purposes.

Now let me share with you why I believe God is still blessing our immoral nation:

1. America's present prosperity is God's last mercy call before his chastening occurs!

Throughout the scriptures, we detect a pattern: Whenever nations turned away from God, he sent them warnings through prophets. If the people didn't respond, God often sent violent storms and drastic weather changes and plagues to wake them up. And if that didn't work, God sent them one final message: he inundated them with prosperity. It was a last, great mercy call!

In most cases, the people despised God's blessings and goodness, turning to indulgence. And when that happened, judgment quickly followed. Paul writes: "...despisest thou the riches of his goodness and forbearance and longsuffering; not knowing that the goodness of God leadeth thee to repentance? But after thy hardness and impenitent heart treasurest up unto thyself wrath against the day of wrath and revelation of the righteous judgment of God; who will render to every man according to his deeds" (Romans 2:4-6).

God is saying, "My day of reckoning is coming upon you. And you know you deserve my wrath and judgment! Yet, by sending you all these present blessings, I mean to woo you to repentance. My goodness to you is meant to reveal your unworthiness and to humble you. But if you continue to despise my blessings and walk in blatant sin, you'll only store up my wrath against you!"

Day after day, our prosperity here in America grows. Yet we have not humbled ourselves. We're storing up God's wrath against us — and soon he'll pour it out!

Let me give you a few examples of societies that prospered just prior to judgment:

Consider the days of Noah — prosperity was the last call!

God determined to judge Noah's society because of its awful violence, pursuit of pleasure and growing wickedness. But first he sent them Noah, a preacher of righteousness, to warn them of coming judgment. And, in his great mercy, God gave that society one hundred and twenty years of wonderful prosperity. Scripture says, "...in the days of Noah...they did eat, they drank, they married...they bought, they sold, they planted, they builded" (Luke 17:26-28). The people feasted, celebrated harvests, had plenty of work, traded their goods. In short, business was booming, with building projects and fine homes being built. Yet the whole time, a cloud of destruction was gathering overhead — and Noah continued to deliver his prophetic warnings.

But the people only ignored Noah and kept indulging their sensuality. They had no time for prophets or warnings of coming judgment. They could only see good times ahead. And their booming prosperity lasted up to the very day of the flood — "...until the day that Noah entered the ark..." (verse 27). On that bright, sunny day, with just a few clouds in the sky, God finally told Noah and his family, "Today, you're to go into the ark." And, in just a few days' time, the Lord's fierce wrath brought everything down!

Consider the days of Lot — prosperity was the last call!

Sodom and Gomorrah enjoyed the same booming economy as Noah's society. Yet, Ezekiel writes, "This was the iniquity of...Sodom, pride, fulness of bread, and abundance of

13

idleness...neither did she strengthen the hand of the poor and needy. And they were haughty..." (Ezekiel 16:49-50). I ask you — doesn't this sound like a description of the United States? These people had an abundance of provision, with no sign of hard times. They were prosperous, with plenty of leisure time on their hands. Still they ignored the poor!

Right now, our government's welfare cutbacks have gone beyond needed reform and have entered into the realm of sin against God. Desperately needy families are being cut off from their last line of help. And yet the rest of our society continues to suck up all the wealth and live in luxury.

The people of Sodom and Gomorrah didn't know their prosperity was God's final mercy call to them. And, suddenly, overnight, the good times ended. Calamity struck in broad daylight — and within twenty-four hours the whole society lay in ruins!

Consider the days of King Josiah — prosperity was the last call!

Josiah was only eighteen years old when God stirred his heart over something he read in the scriptures. Suddenly, the young king saw that his nation had grieved God by their idolatry — and now every sign pointed to coming judgment. He recognized the historic precedents of judgment in God's word — and he cried out, "God's wrath is being stored up against us!" (see 2 Kings 22:11-13).

Desperate for help, Josiah sent emissaries to the prophetess Huldah, saying, "The scriptures tell me we're in danger of God's wrath. What can we do?" Huldah confirmed that God would bring calamity on Israel — and that he wouldn't change his mind: "...Thus saith the Lord God of Israel...Behold, I will bring evil upon this place, and upon the inhabitants...even all the words of the book which the king of Judah hath read: Because they have forsaken me, and have burned incense unto other gods, that they might provoke me to anger...therefore my wrath shall be kindled against this place, and shall not be quenched" (verses 15-17).

In his mercy, God gave Judah a short reprieve. He told Josiah, "Because your heart was tender, and you humbled yourself, you will not be alive when these calamities fall on Judah." So the following years offered no clue as to the awful judgment God was storing up against Judah. Instead, it looked like a great revival was taking place: Josiah tore down idols and pagan temples, drove out witches, ended child sacrifice, wiped out homosexuality and promiscuous sex, and called the entire nation back to the Lord.

During this time, the nation enjoyed great prosperity. All seemed well, with no economic woes and only good times ahead. But when King Josiah died at age thirty-nine, suddenly the revival was exposed as shallow. The people had been half-hearted in their zeal. And even Josiah's own sons, who would inherit the throne, had remained untouched by the revival.

The prophet Jeremiah saw through it all. And he prophesied: "From the thirteenth year of Josiah...even unto this day...the word of the Lord hath come unto me, and I have spoken unto you...Yet ye have not hearkened unto me, saith the Lord...Therefore...I will take from them the voice of mirth, and the voice of gladness...the sound of the millstones [business], and the light of the candle [prosperity]. And this whole land shall be a desolation..." (Jeremiah 25:3-11).

God had been at work the whole time, pouring on the

15

blessings just before he brought judgment. And now he unleashed his wrath on Judah: "...the Lord turned not from the fierceness of his great wrath, wherewith his anger was kindled against Judah, because of all the provocations that Manasseh had provoked him withal. And the Lord said, I will remove Judah also out of my sight..." (23:26-27).

God removed every blessing from Judah. And his judgment fell at the very height of their prosperity!

One of the most convincing evidences of all is found in Jeremiah 44.

Overnight, Judah's good days turned into a hellish nightmare: Overpowering armies flooded Jerusalem, burning the temple and reducing the city to rubble. And the remnant of Israel had to flee for their lives to Egypt. Yet, even after all this calamity, the remnant continued their idolatry, sacrificing to false gods. God's wrath was stirred again — and he warned them through Jeremiah, "You saw the devastation and ruin I brought on Jerusalem because of your wickedness. Now, put away your false gods — or I'll find you in Egypt and consume you even there!"

But the people rebelled. They told Jeremiah, "...we will not hearken unto thee. But we will certainly do whatsoever thing goeth forth out of our own mouth, to burn incense unto the queen of heaven...for then had we plenty of victuals, and were well, and saw no evil. But since we left off to burn incense to the queen of heaven...we have wanted [lacked] all things, and have been consumed by the sword and by famine" (Jeremiah 44:16-18). What an admission! These people acknowledged their past demonic idolatry, their shedding of innocent blood. Yet still they claimed, "God prospered us back then. Life was good. We were well off, with plenty of goods and no trouble."

Jeremiah was aghast at this. He cried, "Are you blind? Don't you understand it was your idolatry that brought you down? God couldn't endure your abominations any longer! You should have been wiped out, destroyed — but he showed you mercy. Those blessings were your last call. Just look around you, at what's happened since then!"

Consider the fall of Babylon — prosperity is the last call!

Revelation 18 predicts a graphic scene of a prosperous society falling under judgment in a single hour. This society is called Babylon — and many theologians have tried to predict who it will be. Some say it will be a revived Rome. Others say it will be a rebuilt version of the literal Babylon in Iraq.

Scripture doesn't make clear who this Babylon will be. To me, it sounds much like New York City, with its Wall Street and the United Nations. The Bible describes it this way: "...the kings of the earth have committed fornication with her, and the merchants of the earth are waxed rich through the abundance of her delicacies [luxuries]....How much she hath glorified herself, and lived deliciously...for she saith in her heart, I sit a queen...and shall see no sorrow" (Revelation 18:3, 7).

Whoever this Babylon is, its unparalleled prosperity is struck with a sudden economic collapse — and all is lost overnight! All the wealthy businessmen who trade with Babylon had thought they'd have another glorious day of profits. Their ships were loaded with goods, waiting to come into port. But the awesome judgment falls quickly! "The kings of the earth...shall...lament for her, when they shall see the smoke of her burning, standing afar off for the fear of her torment, saying, Alas, alas that great city Babylon...for in one hour is thy judgment come. And the merchants of the earth shall weep and mourn over her; for no man buyeth their merchandise any more" (verses 9-11). Their source of economic power is gone — their prosperity vanished in a moment — because God's judgment fell suddenly!

2. American Christians believe our nation is immune to such judgment, due to the large number of praying believers.

Christians who think America won't be judged stand on this single verse: "If my people, which are called by my name, shall humble themselves, and pray, and seek my face, and turn from their wicked ways; then will I hear from heaven, and will forgive their sin, and will heal their land" (2 Chronicles 7:14).

I thank God for this promise. Every dedicated intercessor and prayer warrior is familiar with it. But I ask you: Where is the evidence that America has repented? We haven't humbled ourselves or turned from our wicked ways — no matter how many Christians have prayed! What evidence do we see that our leaders have humbled themselves and repented of their wicked ways? One commentator writes, "We Americans are willing to have scoundrels as our leaders, as long as they give us prosperity. It doesn't matter whether they're adulterers, just as long as they keep the good times rolling." And a recent presidential campaign slogan was, "It's the economy, stupid." In other words: "Prosperity is the only thing that matters."

Good times are the only things on Americans' minds!

Only if we read the rest of the passage in Chronicles can we grasp God's full meaning to us: "But if ye turn away, and forsake my statutes and my commandments...and shall go and serve other gods, and worship them; then will I pluck them up by the roots out of my land which I have given them..." (verses 19-20). The Lord is saying, "If you refuse to repent, the result will be calamity!"

Likewise, God told Jeremiah: "Therefore will I do unto this house, which is called by my name...as I have done to Shiloh. And I will cast you out of my sight, as I have cast out all your brethren, even the whole seed of Ephraim. Therefore pray not thou for this people, neither lift up cry nor prayer for them, neither make intercession to me: for I will not hear thee" (Jeremiah 7:14-16). Do you see what God is saying here? He declares, "The nation has crossed a line — and I won't hear any prayers now on their behalf!"

Beloved, a time comes when people sin so persistently, grieving God so deeply, that a line is crossed. God determines to bring judgment — and no amount of prayer can change it. This happens time after time in scripture — and it is happening in America right now! God says, "I've had enough of your bloodshed, your idolatry, your pushing me out. Go ahead, make your intercession and pleas — but I won't hear any of it!"

I believe South Korea is an example of this. It is one of the most evangelized of all Asian nations. And it has the largest evangelical churches in the world. One Seoul church has more than 500,000 members, and a number of others have over 25,000. And these aren't just nominal believers. They're praying people who gather by the thousands on "prayer mountains" to seek the Lord.

South Korea also has been one of the most prosperous nations in Asia. It has enjoyed a booming economy — the eleventh largest in the world — with its goods exported worldwide. Bankers from wealthy nations raced there to loan them billions and fan the flames of prosperity. And soon the country became rich beyond all dreams, with full employment. Some observers said South Korea's economy even rivaled Japan's. But overnight, the unthinkable happened: South Korea's monetary unit nearly collapsed — and hundreds of businesses and major industries went bankrupt. The government almost folded, and massive unemployment loomed ahead. An international monetary fund had to rush in with billions of dollars to save the nation from total ruin.

How could this have happened? Did South Korea cross a line of persistent wickedness and idolatry — or did their ruin come because they did not feed the starving masses in North Korea? They are an example to America about what could happen here overnight!

God told Israel: "But go ye now unto my place which was in Shiloh, where I set my name at the first, and see what I did to it for the wickedness of my people Israel" (verse 12). Likewise, God is saying to America, "Consider South Korea, Russia, Indonesia, Bosnia — all the nations that are in economic turmoil. Take warning from their examples!"

In the next chapter, you'll see how God begins his judgments upon a nation by bringing down its economy.

The Crippling of the American Economy

CHAPTER TWO

Not long ago, I listened to a radio talk show on which the guest was a liberal politician. To my amazement, this man made the following statement:

"America is racing toward ruin! Our country is morally crippled. Any thinking citizen can see we're sinking into a mire of degradation beyond all comprehension. We elect people to our highest offices knowing they're liars, adulterers, immoral and two-faced. We Americans seem to be saying, 'Just give us a good economy. We want to be left alone with our videos, VCRs and stereos. We want time and money to eat, drink and enjoy ourselves. So, give us any leader who'll provide all this for us. It doesn't matter if he's a scoundrel — as long as we can prosper!'"

Many Americans — including Christians — see our country as an island of abundant prosperity and endless security. They firmly believe America can't be affected by the economic turmoil and disasters we see falling on other nations around the world. Even many economists today voice such thoughts. They write in the *Wall Street Journal* and the *New York Times,* "America is too strong to be affected by the failing economies of Asia, Russia and other nations. We have too many safe-guards in place. Now we can survive on our own if neces-sary. The problems we're seeing in Asia are just a few glitches along the road."

What arrogance — what blindness! The fact is, the Bible says something completely different about nations like ours. Let me share it with you:

The Bible warns that when God pours out his judgments on nations, he begins by crippling the economy!

"Behold, this was the iniquity of thy sister Sodom, pride, fulness of bread, and abundance of idleness...neither did she strengthen the hand of the poor and needy. And they were haughty and committed abomination before me: therefore I took them away as I saw good" (Ezekiel 16:49-50).

The prophet Ezekiel is describing a time of lewdness and abominations in Israel that was beyond his comprehension. He told the people, "You've become far more wicked than Sodom! You've committed even greater abominations than that evil society. You're marked by shame and disgrace!" (see verses 53-58). Ezekiel also made it clear that God would move in judgment on Israel at a precise time — and he would bring down their boom-ing prosperity!

I wonder how Ezekiel would react today if he were to walk the streets of our cities and observe all the wealth and prosperity we're experiencing. I believe that holy man would be speechless! He'd be shocked by all the arrogance, the ha-tred toward God, the materialism, the flaunting of sins, the militant homosexuality, the crime and drugs. He probably would cry, "America, you're more abominable than Sodom! You're even more wicked than backslidden, idolatrous Israel. In fact, you're the proudest, most ungrateful society in history! You've gone far past the flash point at which God moved against Israel and Sodom. And the first thing God is going to do to you is to strike your prosperity. He'll humble you as he has all other nations who forsook him!"

Ezekiel's prophecies of judgment upon Israel were lost in the hustle and bustle of that society's prosperity. Jerusalem and her sister cities were caught up in trading, building, feasting, enjoying the good life. They had "fullness of bread" — that is, plenty of goods — and an abundance of free time for recreation and idleness. And they were proud of their luxurious lifestyle. To them, Ezekiel's warnings seemed completely out of touch with reality. Some of them even thought of his preaching as entertainment. They mocked him, saying to each other, "Let's go down and listen to that wild preacher!"

But the truth was, God already had a date set — a specific hour — at which he would cripple Israel's economy and lifestyle: "It came to pass in the ninth year of his reign, in the tenth month, in the tenth day of the month, that Nebuchadnezzar king of Babylon came...against Jerusalem...and built forts against it round about" (Jeremiah 52:4). Suddenly, in a time of great prosperity, Israel was surrounded by Nebuchadnezzar and his mighty Chaldean army. Overnight, the Israelites' lifestyle changed completely!

In a modern setting, this passage would read something like, "In the last year of President So-and-so's second term, on October 10th, God laid siege on the American economy and lifestyle..." That's just how precise God is in his judgments! He has a time clock for all of his actions. And he has already marked the day when he'll move against America's economy and our lifestyle — and nothing can change that set time!

Let me give you a glimpse of what I'm talking about: On October 18, 1987, during a Sunday morning service at Times Square Church, I warned our congregation that the stock market was about to be hit hard. I'd felt a tremendous stirring in my heart from the Lord about this matter. God had whispered to me, "David, if you want to see a picture of what my judgment will look like, go down to Wall Street tomorrow." I told our congregation about it and invited anyone who wanted to accompany me.

On the very next day — Monday, October 19 — several of us stood on the steps of the stock exchange and waited. When trading finished that day, the market had fallen 508 points — a full one-fourth of its value! (By comparison, in today's market — January 1998 — this would equal a 3,000-point dive.) And it all happened in just a few hours! As the shocked traders exited, we saw the panic on their faces. They muttered, "There goes my condo, my boat! How on earth did that happen? What's going on? And when will it end?" It was chaotic.

An editorial in the *New York Daily News* from that week read: "Yesterday's plunge of the stock market continues — and now Americans want to know why. What happened? Why didn't someone tell us these bad things were going to happen?"

Finally, one commentator wrote that it was all due to a "materialistic society, an irresponsible government, and a 'Me Generation' that wouldn't listen. In plain language, the United States has been living far beyond its means over the past five years. Total consumption by households, businesses and government has exceeded our income by almost $500 billion of debt. So now we're in the soup, the chickens have come home to roost, and the hangover from our party is here." If a preacher had written this, people would have laughed. But it came from an economist — an expert on Wall Street!

Now God has appointed a specific day and hour to make his move of judgment. We don't know how soon it will take place. But we do know from scripture that this time there will be no mercy — no quick rebound! I picture the President calling an emergency meeting of his Cabinet leaders and demanding, "How did this happen? What went wrong?" The officials in that room will merely sit in stony silence. No one will know how to stop the economy's hemorrhaging!

This will be God's way of saying, "You've ignored me for this long — now, let someone else tell you how to escape your mess. You don't want me in your courts, your schools, your society. So, go ahead — turn to your experts and stargazers!"

If you think my warnings of coming judgment seem too harsh, read these words from a well-known, syndicated columnist in the *New York Post*. He wrote on December 31, 1997:

"We have seen Asian stock-market declines of 40 to 60 percent, and commensurate collapses in currency values. These losses translate into business failures, job layoffs in the millions, and Asian factories auctioned off at fire-sale prices to U.S. bidders — a splendid formula for anti-American nationalist backlash....

"Indonesia is on the brink of bankruptcy. An economic storm is gathering and spreading over Hong Kong and mainland China. Japan is in critical shape, its banks and industries falling into bankruptcies. Real estate prices are off 80 percent. And the stock market is off 65 percent from its peak....

"South Korea cannot survive without a $30 billion bailout from the international monetary fund. Millions face unemployment. Banks and institutions are lying idle and closing....

"Russia is in the worst condition of all. The country may default on its astronomical debt. The economy is in shambles. There are food shortages, and workers are not being paid....

"The United States seems remarkably unaffected thus far. Predictions of happy days persist. But three things are now clear: Something is horribly amiss with the global economy. There is not enough money left to cover all the disasters and blunders. And the President's luck — and ours — may soon run out."

Again, this is no preacher writing — but an economic expert!

The book of Lamentations is Jeremiah's cry after God smote Israel with judgments.

When Jeremiah wrote Lamentations, judgment had already fallen on Israel, Judah and Jerusalem. The nation's cities and temples lay in ruins. Within just a short time, Israel had gone from a booming prosperity to this description:

"All her people sigh, they seek bread; they have given their pleasant things for meat to relieve the soul...the young children ask bread, and no man breaketh it unto them. They that did feed delicately are desolate in the streets: they that were brought up in scarlet embrace dunghills" (Lamentations 1:11, 4:4-5).

"...there is no more bread in the city" (Jeremiah 38:9).

God absolutely crushed their economy! Jeremiah lamented, "The kings of the earth...would not have believed that the adversary and the enemy should have entered into the gates of Jerusalem. For the sins of her prophets, and the iniquities of her priests, that have shed the blood of the just in the midst of her..." (Lamentations 4:12-13). In other words: "The kings of the earth are shocked and amazed! Who would have believed such prosperity would end overnight?"

The economy in the Old Testament often was identified with bread. The prophet Isaiah used this image to describe God's coming judgment upon Israel: "Behold, the Lord...doth take away from Jerusalem and from Judah the stay and the staff [the stock and store], the whole stay [supply] of bread..." (Isaiah 3:1). Isaiah was saying, "God has stopped all your commerce. And he's taken away all your storehouses of bread. All the things you hoarded and piled up are now gone!" The prophet went on to warn that the value of gold and silver would totally collapse. People would end up casting their gold and silver into the streets as worthless, or trading them for a mere morsel of food.

Beloved, it was all because God smote their economy. And we dare not think such things can't happen in America! You may try to turn off all these warnings — to close your ears and say it's all just doom-saying — but I tell you from the depths of my soul: Financial calamity is going to strike America — soon!

Think about it: How can God judge South Korea — with its millions of intercessors and great missionary churches — and yet spare America, which now spends more money on dog food than it does on missions? Millions of people are starving to death in North Korea — yet not even that nation allows its babies to be aborted with the intensity and arrogance that the United States does. Nor does it allow any pornography. It has not sinned as grossly as America has. So, I ask you: How can God spare us from such judgments?

I believe God is saying to us right now: "America, look at what has happened to South Korea! Look at Japan, Russia — all the nations around you who are teetering on the brink of an economic holocaust. Now your time has come!"

America is on the brink of an economic holocaust!

The global markets are the most powerful forces in the world today. The average daily worldwide trading in financial transactions now exceeds $1 trillion — mostly by high financial institutions looking for only short-term profits. Yet this vast ocean of money, flowing unregulated, has resulted in an electronic force that could spin out of control in a matter of hours. There is now the daily risk of a chain reaction causing an economic meltdown and plunging the world into financial chaos. Personally, I believe we're going to see a meltdown of our bond markets.

In June 1997, these same global forces brought down the thriving Asian Rim nations. After years of unparalleled prosperity and growth, the "miracle of the Asian tigers" suddenly ended. Those economies that were considered nearly invincible suddenly were shattered overnight — first in Thailand, then in Malaysia, then in Indonesia and South Korea. Some currencies lost 70 percent of their value within days. And when the Hong Kong stock market began to plunge, the world markets became very nervous. Many experts believed a worldwide economic meltdown was about to happen.

The International Monetary Fund (IMF) pledged over $120 billion of emergency funds to stop the plunge, as national treasuries ran out of funds. But these huge commitments to Asia quickly depleted the IMF funds — and any financial crisis in South America could destabilize the global picture.

Simply put, America is no longer in control of her economic future. We are now subject to the unprecedented financial power of world markets — a force that dwarfs that of this nation. Anyone who believes the United States is immune to the risks of foreign markets is blind and misinformed. And now the world's financial markets are in deep trouble. Right now, massive unemployment is crippling the Asian Rim nations even more. And time is running out!

America is receiving her last call to repent before God's chastening comes — and it is a prosperity call! Not long ago, a New York City newspaper published a cartoon picturing the Titanic leaving port. The ship was renamed "The U.S. Economy." And above the ship were these words: "Not even God can sink this ship!" Yet the U.S. ambassador to Japan recently warned America against becoming smug about our economy. He told the *New York Times,* "The United States ought to remember the biblical injunction — pride goeth before destruction...a haughty spirit before a fall."

I tell you, the American dream is going to turn into the American nightmare! It will happen suddenly, without warning — and no one will be able to explain how or why it happened. There will be sellers only, with no buyers in sight!

A majority of Americans have concluded, "Morals do not

count. Let our leaders do as they please. Just give us a boom-ing economy. Let the good times roll! All that matters is pros-perity." But God is about to crush this abominable American mindset! And, like the prophet Jeremiah, we who believe in the holy, righteous judgments of God will say, "The Lord hath done that which he had devised; he hath fulfilled his word that he had commanded in the days of old..." (Lamentations 2:17).

In the next chapter, I'll prove to you from scripture how God responds when a nation crosses a line — sinning away its day of grace!

America Has Crossed the Line

CHAPTER THREE

I have never claimed to be a prophet. But there comes a time when the word of God becomes such a fire in my bones, I have to speak out what I see and hear. Call it a watchman's message, or whatever you will — but I have to tell you what God has put on my heart concerning this nation!

I do believe God has true prophets — those who are occasionally moved upon by the Holy Spirit to foretell future events and coming judgments. Indeed, on a few occasions, the Spirit has compelled me to warn of impending judgments. But the prophecy I bring you now is not predictive. Rather, I want to take you straight into God's Word, to show you a few eternal principles of how the Lord works. As I have previously stated, we can know the future by studying the past!

The fact is, God's ways are absolutely unchangeable when it comes to his dealings with sinful nations. There is no shadow of turning in his ways; he works the same way in every generation — because he is just. In short, he will deal with our generation in the same way he has dealt with every other generation that sinned as we are sinning. And by learning these principles of his ways from scripture, we can deduct exactly how he will deal with us today.

For example: The apostle Paul predicted to the Corinthian church what would happen to them if they continued to tempt Christ. Those Christians were murmuring and giving themselves over to unbridled lusts. So, Paul simply looked into history and saw what God did to Israel when they committed the very same sins. Paul told the Corinthians: "Neither let us tempt Christ, as some of them also tempted, and were destroyed of serpents. Neither murmur ye, as some of them also murmured, and were destroyed of the destroyer. Now all these things happened unto them for ensamples: and they are written for our admonition, upon whom the ends of the world are come" (1 Corinthians 10:9-11). The apostle was saying, "This is a clear pattern in scripture. It tells you what God will do to you if you continue to sin as Israel sinned!"

The apostle Peter also warned his readers by invoking an example from the Old Testament. He said God would judge them for their covetousness and unbridled lust, just as he had judged past generations: "And turning the cities of Sodom and Gomorrha into ashes [God] condemned them with an overthrow, making them an ensample unto those that after would live ungodly" (2 Peter 2:6). Peter warned, "If you sin as Sodom and Gomorrha did, the Lord will destroy you just as he destroyed them!"

Like Paul and Peter, I bring you a warning based on my study of the Old Testament — specifically, the book of Isaiah. As I read through this book recently, the Spirit stopped me in chapter 22. Suddenly, I began to see how judgment came upon Jerusalem in Isaiah's day — in spite of all of the prophet's warnings. This chapter contains a shocking account of a society that had sinned away its day of grace. Jerusalem and

Judah had crossed a line — and there was no turning back. The people had backslidden completely and were living as though they were atheists. So God instructed Isaiah to prophesy to his people — to pronounce a "dread release" to judgment!

You see, God's call to repentance in Judah was over. There would no longer be a prophetic voice in the land, crying, "Return and be healed!" Now it was too late. This people had done something so brazen, God could not endure it one more day. And so, tearfully, with a crushed heart, Isaiah brought this awful message: "And it was revealed in mine ears by the Lord of hosts, Surely this iniquity shall not be purged from you till ye die, saith the Lord God of hosts" (Isaiah 22:14). He was saying, in essence, "YOU'VE COMMITTED A SIN THAT GOD WON'T FORGIVE. YOU'VE CROSSED A LINE — AND IT'S TOO LATE TO TURN BACK!"

When you fully understand what this society did to provoke God to release them to judgment, you will see how their actions mirror American society today.

What Jerusalem and Judah did to bring judgment upon themselves is exactly what America is doing right now. And if the wicked behavior of God's people signaled the imminent destruction of that society, then our sinful behavior clearly signals judgment on our nation. Indeed, if the prophet Isaiah were living today, beholding the wickedness of our nation, he would cry out, "It's time to weep for your nation! History is repeating itself. Your cup of iniquity is full and overflowing!"

Chapter 22 of Isaiah is called "The Valley of Vision." And

Isaiah's message here is so clear, so easy to understand, there can be no doubt about its meaning. According to commentators, Isaiah was evidently standing on a rooftop or some other high elevation, looking over Jerusalem and the surrounding valley. What he saw was so appalling, it broke him. He wept convulsively, saying to all who passed by, "...Look away from me; I will weep bitterly, labour not to comfort me, because of the spoiling of the daughter of my people" (verse 4). The prophet was saying, "Don't look at me. You won't like what you see! My heart is about to break, and my insides are about to pour out. I'm sorely pained, and I can't take it. My people are about to be destroyed!" "My heart panted, fearfulness affrighted me...my loins [are] filled with pain...I was bowed down... dismayed..." (21:4, 3).

This clearly was not patriotism on Isaiah's part. It was the burden of the Lord! Here is a picture of a man broken over his society's sin — something we don't often see in the church today. There simply aren't many pastors or Christians in America who see judgment coming and who are broken over it.

Yet, for a long time, Isaiah had been speaking of a vision of judgment he had received from the Lord. He had foreseen a huge army — a contingent of chariots, cunning archers, powerful horsemen, men on camels — all coming against the city. And now, Isaiah's prophetic vision was unfolding before his very eyes. Enemy armies had surrounded Jerusalem — and a siege was under way! The noise of military movements echoed over the hills: The terrible, famed horsemen of Elam and hand-to-hand fighters of Kir were marching in the vanguard. War horses groaned and grunted, their hooves pounding the earth. Chariot wheels rumbled over the countryside, churning up great clouds of dust. Infantrymen had approached

Jerusalem's wall, and now they were noisily picking away at it with their spears and crowbars. It must have been a fearful, awesome sight!

As Isaiah turned from this frightful scene, he looked upon the flat rooftops of the city — and he could not believe what he saw. The citizens of Jerusalem were on the rooftops — drinking and partying! The people had gathered to entertain themselves by gazing down on the Assyrian army as it prepared to attack. Isaiah was incredulous at what he saw — and he cried out, "Thou that art full of stirs, a tumultuous city, a joyous city..." (22:2). Prior to this time, the prophet had been walking up and down the land, warning God's people, "Your idols will be brought down. The city walls in which you trusted will be breached. Your glory shall fade. Time is running out!"

Yet, how did the people react? They jostled each other on the rooftops, trying to get the best view of the approaching enemy! The whole city was stirred up, full of excitement and curiosity. The Bible uses a word here that means "boisterous, loud, excited." People whose dwellings were closest to the wall had good views of the valley below, and they hosted their friends for "viewing parties." They cried, "Come on up — you've got to see this. Pack your lunch and bring the family!" Children screamed with delight: "Look at all the big white horses! Look at all the sleek chariots, and the mighty soldiers oiling their shields. What a sight!"

They were feasting, getting drunk, celebrating. And Isaiah could not contain himself. He cried out: "...What aileth thee now, that thou art wholly gone up to the housetops?" (verse 1). I can see this prophet of God in my mind's eye, screaming from the rooftop: "Are you people crazy? What kind of spirit has possessed you? What kind of madness would drive you to your rooftops to party, while destruction sits at your gates? Judgment is at the door — and you're getting drunk!"

I have a question for you: What ails our American society? How can our whole nation party, dance, drink and be saturated with entertainment, while thousands of babies are being aborted? What kind of disease has so blinded our nation that the President could veto a bill outlawing doctors from sucking out the brains of babies just weeks before they're born? What horrible sickness allows our society to continue merrily in its sordid pleasure-seeking, while the elderly are being assisted in suicide? America is under siege by an army of abortionists, pornographers, drug pushers, murderers of the elderly, coming at us from all corners of the earth. And yet, only a few prophetic voices can be heard!

I'm sure Isaiah's voice was drowned out by the partying crowds: "Oh, it's only that old man, Isaiah — the gloom-and-doom preacher. Don't pay any attention to him." And so it is today: Prophetic warnings are ridiculed and ignored!

I ask you: where are those who grieve for America — who are broken over the sins of God's church and our nation?

Consider that stupid, blind, stoned rooftop crowd in Jerusalem, celebrating on the brink of their own judgment! Beloved, this is where you discover the flash point of judgment! What was their sin, which God would not forgive? It was much more than just shutting out God's warnings. Their sin was hardening their hearts in the face of the predicted judgment!

Judgment was already taking place; it was evident all around them. And still the people hardened themselves, know-

ing full well the hand of God had brought down this judgment upon them. Their hardness was the unforgivable sin!
Yet Isaiah was further incredulous: Not only were the people
mocking judgment at the door, being entertained by it — but
they were celebrating and feasting in the midst of a plague!

People were falling dead because a plague had swept the
city: "...thy slain men are not slain with the sword, nor dead in
battle" (verse 2). Historians confirm that Jerusalem was hit by a
plague at this time. Refugees had fled there before the invading
army, crowding into a city with little food and water. Health
conditions were awful, resulting in the plague. People began
dying left and right. The stench of death was horrible. But the
citizens of Jerusalem became accustomed to the plague. They
became hardened to the death all around them — so much so
that they could entertain themselves on rooftops while just
below them people were dying. They carelessly wasted the
city's scarce water, food and wine on their own pleasure!

I ask you — doesn't this sound awfully familiar? It is a
picture of America, in this generation! We have become like
Germany just before that nation fell in World War II. I have a
history book at home with vivid photographs of the drunken
parties that took place throughout Berlin. Hitler was in his bun-
ker, close to suicide, as Allied forces made nightly bombing
raids. Yet in between the waves of bombs, people rushed out
to makeshift bars, to dance and drink the night away. Berlin
became one massive party. And it all happened just before the
city was annihilated — with the people staring into eternity!

Even now, here in New York City, fund-raising for AIDS
research consists mainly of all-night dancing and drinking parties. I see posters all over Greenwich Village and Soho that
read: "AIDS Research Party. Free drinks." They dance the

night away, racing from one party to another — all in the name of raising money for AIDS research. They're dying of the disease — but they go on partying!

Right now an AIDS plague is spreading throughout America. But I believe something even worse could happen to this nation — because of something I see in Isaiah 22. Suppose the awful, flesh-eating disease called ebola strikes with a fury in America. (This is the flesh-eating disease that can kill a person within a week.) Or perhaps one of the newly discovered, exotic diseases begins to snuff out life in mere days. Thousands of Americans would begin dying quickly. Our country would be as it was during the nineteenth century, when small pox raged through the streets. During that awful plague, people fled the cities. But after a while, when the sight of funerals and hearses became commonplace, the people grew inured to it all.

If such an outbreak were to decimate the United States today, do you think our nation would turn to God? Would we wake up and repent? Would the ungodly cry out for mercy and healing? No! On the contrary — America would be swamped with the most wild, unbelievable orgies and parties in the history of our nation. Indeed, that has been the history of every nation that turned from God as we have.

As everything neared collapse in Jerusalem, the rich and influential made provisions to flee to safety: "All thy rulers are fled together...all that are found in thee are bound together, which have fled from afar...." (Isaiah 22:3). Those seeking to flee were leaders, people "in the know." And they knew Isaiah was right — that society had reached a point of no return: "For it is a day of trouble, and of treading down, and of perlexity by the Lord God of hosts in the valley of vision, breaking down the walls, and of crying to the mountains" (verse 5).

These people raced about, looking to make one last financial "kill" by which they could secure themselves against society's breakdown. Their attitude was, "I've got to make a bundle quickly. Then I'll find a safe, secure place to hide." Yet Isaiah knew exactly what they were up to. He pointed out that the city treasurer, Shebna, "...heweth him out a sepulchre on high, and that graveth an habitation for himself in a rock..." (verse 16). The prophet was saying, "Look! Your city treasurer is up in the hills, building himself a rock shelter. He says it's a sepulchre — but he's going up there to hide!"

Beloved, that is the American dream for multitudes right now! The saying among Wall Streeters, businesspeople and politicians today is, "Give me a golden parachute!" In other words: "Make a killing — and then head for the hills!" Think about it: Why are so many wealthy people buying up isolated ranches and farms in Utah, Nevada, Wyoming, Montana, New England? What do they know that the majority of Americans don't know? They see the enemy gathering at the gate! They know America can no longer carry out its suicidal economic policies without crashing. This is not simply a gut feeling on their part; they know the end of the boom is near. They may be partying, but they're also preparing!

Yet there is no safe place to hide. Isaiah said to the unscrupulous escapees in Jerusalem: "He will surely violently turn and toss thee like a ball into a large country: there shalt thou die, and there the chariots of thy glory shall be the shame of thy lord's house. And I will drive thee from thy station, and from thy state shall he pull thee down" (verses 18-19). In other words: "God is going to find you in hiding and bring you out into the open. There is no safe place outside of Jesus Christ the Lord!"

God, in his mercy, made one
last attempt to save Jerusalem.

The Lord sent his Spirit upon the people while they were partying. Suddenly, their eyes were opened to the danger they were in: "And he discovered the covering of Judah..." (verse 8). We are not told exactly what happened when the Holy Spirit came down and interrupted the party. We don't know if anyone went to the temple to pray, or if anyone went to Isaiah and asked what to do. But there probably was a brief period when people at least thought of God and said a few prayers. Deep inside, they knew God's hand was in this judgment.

Perhaps you remember a similar scene in our nation a few years ago. When the war with Iraq broke out, it was reported that President Bush spent hours praying with Billy Graham. Congress called for a national day of prayer. Churches were packed. Even the newspapers in New York City called for prayer. Yet, this lasted all of one week! What happened? The same thing happened in our nation as had happened in Jerusalem: "...thou didst look in that day to the armour..." (same verse).

When the Lord exposed the people of Jerusalem to danger, they should have turned to him. Instead, they turned to their own resources — the strength of their armor! They told themselves, "We have good, sturdy shields. And the city wall is strong. We have all the materials we need to fill the breaches. We can fortify ourselves." Simply put, they didn't need God!

And that is just how we reacted during the Gulf War. Television provided daily reports on the mighty exploits of our military. We watched as U.S. tanks rumbled swiftly through the desert, overwhelming the enemy. We watched in awe as our planes shot off laser-beam bombs, hitting pinpoint targets. One general boasted, "We're capable of putting a missile down any smokestack in Iraq!" And it all ended with a ticker-tape parade down Broadway. Yet, was it to honor God, to whom we prayed? No — it was for our generals! God was pushed out of the picture completely.

I am not belittling our military. Of course, I thank God they were successful. And I thank God for the soldiers who served our country so well. But the fact remains that America trusts more in its military might than in almighty God! "...but ye have not looked unto the maker thereof, neither had respect unto him that fashioned it long ago" (verse 11). This is why Isaiah wept so hard over Israel. A false security had gripped the people, and God was no longer even in their thoughts. Instead, everyone clung to a brazen self-confidence that said, "We will go it alone!"

America today is caught in the deception of a similar false security. The Russian empire has fallen. Iraq has been defeated. And now we think, "Who is strong enough to challenge our mighty army? There is no one left to challenge us. There is no longer a hydrogen scare." We have trusted in our armor! But we'd better beware — because Russia is not dead! The bear that the Bible said would be wounded will come back to life. And that Russian bear is stirring right now. I don't know whether it will happen by coup or by election — but the two or three men who are in line for leadership in Russia are all anti-Christian, anti-Semitic and anti-American. The Russian threat is still very dangerous.

These men who will come to power shortly will not be afraid to threaten America or the world. They will not take their finger off the hydrogen button. And right now, the Russian army is licking its wounds, itching to remove its shame before the world. Once it is finally in power, it may attempt to conquer its former states — and could then be a threat to Europe. A dictator is going to arise overnight — a man who is anti-Semitic. Hitler rose up out of chaos, and so will a new, belligerent Russia. Just watch, as emissaries from all over the world start flocking to Moscow. Don't be deceived by the relative peace our nation now enjoys. It is merely the calm before the storm!

What triggers God's dread release of a society to judgment?

What final indignation, what brazen act, sets God's judgment into motion? What was Israel's iniquity that triggered judgment? What made God say, "That's enough. Now you've crossed the line!" Isaiah gives us the answer: "And in that day did the Lord God of hosts call to weeping, and to mourning, and to baldness, and to girding with sackcloth; And behold joy and gladness, slaying oxen, and killing sheep, eating flesh, and drinking wine: let us eat and drink; for to morrow we shall die" (verses 12-13). Even in the midst of their brazen rebellion, God's Spirit was calling people to repentance. The holy cry was heard in the streets: "Weep, mourn, put on sackcloth!"

But instead of mourning, the people partied on! Instead of grieving and weeping, they reveled with food and wine. They reasoned, "By this time tomorrow we'll all be dead. Why should we save any of the livestock? Let's slay all the sheep and have one final, gluttonous feast. Quick — bring out the wine barrels. We'll go out stoned!"

So they danced and drank on the rooftops, watching as the enemy moved into place: Chariots lined up in row after row. Battering rams rolled into position. Legions of cavalrymen stood battle ready. Already, breaches were being made in the wall. In just a few more hours, it would all be over. The citizens of Jerusalem knew they were going to die — that they were facing eternity. I would like to tell you that at the hour of the reality of death, the people flocked to the temple to pray. I would like to tell you that they sought out Isaiah, begging him to tell them how to change God's mind and remove the enemy from their gates. But they didn't! Fatalism had already taken over — and the people preferred to face death as atheists!

They had crossed the line, with no reprieve possible. Now, no amount of mercy, fear or warnings could move them. It was as if they lifted their wine glasses in a toast to God and laughed in his face: "Here's to you, God. See you in hell!" This was the final indignity against God — the trigger of judgment! And, beloved, the very same attitude is rampant in America today. Our nation is characterized by what has been called the "sensuality of despair." The thinking is, "I know I'm going to hell. But I don't want God in my face!"

America has stuck its nose up at God!

You ask, "Why such a message? It sounds so gloomy!"

Perhaps you're thinking, "Brother Dave, I don't know how to react when I read this. I feel so downcast." No! That isn't the reaction of one who is prepared to go home to be with the

Lord. Dying is a promotion. Jesus lovingly told us that when we see these things beginning to happen, we are to look up and rejoice — because our redemption is drawing close! There is no need to be afraid. God hasn't given us a spirit of fear about such things, but a spirit of power, love and a sound mind. Look up — your savior is drawing near!

Now, we'll look at how God responds to nations that shed the blood of the just and innocent.

Mayday for the Shedding of the Blood of Innocents

There is one thing that's as certain as night and day: When stately nations, populous societies or booming cities shed the blood of the just and the innocent, God turns them into ruinous heaps! Over the past few decades alone, America has shed the blood of multiplied millions of innocent babies. God's word says the blood of these innocents is precious in his sight (see Psalm 116:15). Scripture warns that the cries of their blood reach high into the heavens, demanding justice. Indeed, every drop of blood of every aborted child in this land cries out for justice. And God promises to punish the nation that is responsible: "...thou hast given them blood to drink; for they are worthy" (Revelation 16:6).

The Bible also warns that God curses all who shed the blood of the just — in the same way he cursed Cain, the first shedder of innocent blood: "...the voice of thy brother's blood crieth unto me from the ground. And now art thou cursed from the earth, which hath opened her mouth to receive thy brother's blood from thy hand" (Genesis 4:10-11). We can be assured that not a single baby's slaughter will go unnoticed by our God of justice. He promises to "...(make) inquisition for blood...he remembereth them: he forgetteth not the cry of the humble" (Psalm 9:12).

God has sworn to judge and cut off every nation that condemns its innocents to death.

"They gather themselves together against the soul of the righteous, and condemn the innocent blood" (Psalm 94:21). "And he shall bring upon them their own iniquity, and shall cut them off in their own wickedness; yea, the Lord our God shall cut them off" (verse 23).

History offers abundant proof that God cuts off those who shed innocent blood, especially the blood of his martyrs and innocents (babies). And history confirms these biblical warnings. The ancient historian Eusebius gives these accounts of the judgments that befell Israel's succession of Herods, as well as Caiaphas, the high priest who condemned Christ to death:

"Herod the Great, who caused the babes of Bethlehem to be slain, hoping thereby to have destroyed Christ, shortly after was plagued by God with an incurable disease, having a slow and slack fire continually tormenting of his inward parts; he had a vehement and greedy desire to eat, and yet nothing would satisfy him; his inward bowels rotted, his breath was short and stinking, some of his members rotted, and in all his members he had so violent a cramp, that nature was not able to bear it, and so, growing mad with pain, he died miserably.

"Herod Antipas, who beheaded John the Baptist, not long after, falling into disgrace with the Roman emperor, with his incestuous Herodias, the suggester of that murder, they were banished, and fell into such misery and poverty that they ended their wretched lives with much shame and misery.

"Herod Agrippa was a great persecutor of the saints...he was eaten up of worms in the third year of his reign, as Josephus observes. He went to Caesarea to keep certain plays in honour of Caesar...and when he had made an end of his starched oration in this his bravery, his flatterers extolled him as a god, crying out, It is the voice of a god, and not of a man, whereupon he was presently smitten by the angel of the Lord, and so died with worms that ate up his bowels...they separated his wretched soul from his loathsome body within...five days.

"Caiaphas the high priest, who gathered the council, and suborned false witness against the Lord Christ, was shortly after put out of his office...whereupon he killed himself. Not long after Pontius Pilate had condemned our Lord Christ, he lost his deputyship and Caesar's favor; and being fallen into disgrace with the Roman emperor, and banished by him, he fell into such misery that he hanged himself."

God inflicts dreadful judgments on the chief blood-shedders of persecutors of Christians.

Here is a further account from history detailing how God has kept his promise to "cut off" and bring judgment on those who slaughter the righteous and innocent:

"Nero, that monster of men, who raised the first bloody persecution, to pick a quarrel with the Christians, he set the city of Rome on fire, and then charged it upon them; under which pretence he exposes them to the fury of the people, who cruelly tormented them, as if they had been common burners and destroyers of cities, and the deadly enemies of mankind; yea, Nero himself caused them to be apprehended and clad in wild beasts' skins, and torn in pieces with dogs;

47

others were crucified, some he made bonfires of to light him in his night-sports. To be short, such horrid cruelty he used towards them, as caused many of their enemies to pity them. But God found out this wretched persecutor at last; for being adjudged by the senate an enemy to mankind, he was condemned to be whipped to death for the prevention whereof he cut his own throat.

"Domitian, the author of the second persecution against the Christians, having drawn a catalogue of such as he was to kill, in which was the name of his own wife and other friends; upon which he was, by the consent of his wife, slain by his own household servants with daggers in his privy-chamber; his body was buried without honour, his memory cursed to posterity, and his arms and ensigns were thrown down and defaced.

"Trajan raised the third persecution against the church; he was continually vexed with seditions, and the vengeance of God followed him close. For, first, he fell into a palsy, then lost the use of his senses; afterwards he fell into a dropsy, and died in great anguish.

"Adrian being vexed with great and perpetual commotions in his life, died with much anxiety.

"Maximinus being declared an enemy by the senate, was killed in his own tent.

"Decius, by the Goths, in their first invasion of the empire, with his whole army was cut off.

"Valerianus was overcome by the Persians, and made use of by Sapor as a stirrup for his foot when he went to take horse.

"Julian, in his height of contempt against Christ, was deadly wounded in battle against the Persians, and throwing his blood in the air, died with (a) desperate expression in his mouth...

"Valentius, being a great favourer of the Arians, and a great persecutor of the orthodox — the Arians exceeding the heathens in cruelty — was in battle against the Goths in Thracia wounded, and being carried to a house that was near, it was set on fire by the enemy, in which he miserably perished.

"Maxentius and his chief officers being put to flight on the other side of the river Tiber, by Constantine, was necessitated to return by a bridge, whereupon he had made devices in a secret way to have drowned Constantine, by which he and those that were with him were drowned in the river; upon which occasion the Christians took occasion to sing that word, Psalm 9:16, 'The Lord is known by the judgments which he executeth: the wicked is snared in the work of his own hand': and that word, Psalm 7:15, 'He made a pit and digged it, and he himself is fallen into it.'

"Diocesan being sent for by Constantine, upon suspicion, chose rather to poison himself than to see him.

"Maximinus Herculeus, endeavouring again to recover his authority, was discovered in his design by his daughter, Constantine's wife: whereupon he was pursued and besieged by Constantine, and was either killed, or during the siege hanged himself, as is diversely reported by several writers.

"Maximinus Jovius, through intemperance, becoming corpulent, was smitten with boils in the secret parts, out of which issued abundance of vermin; his physicians were either suffocated by the odious smell of his loathsome disease, or else they were killed by him because they could not cure him. (One of his physicians told him that it was God's judgment on him for persecuting the Christians, which no man could cure.) At last he fell under such convictions, as forced him to confess that the wrongs and injuries that he had done to the people of God were the cause of that plague; and therefore being struck with terror and horror, gave out edicts that the persecution should cease, and that churches should be builded, and that in their meetings prayers should be put up for him, as formerly used to be: which edict is to be found in Eusebius. The other tyrant in the east, to wit, Maximinus, who was called Caesar, had been industrious to invent cruel tortures for the Christians, especially to pull out their eyes; but at last he was defeated, and in a base habit made to hide himself, and afterwards he was pursued by such a sickness which made both his eyes to drop out of his head, by which judgment he was necessitated to confess that the God of the Christians was the only true God, and that he had been mistaken concerning the gods whom he close to worship; which words were uttered by him when he was even expiring, as Eusebius testifies. By all these dreadful instances, you may run and read that heavy vengeance that has been inflicted upon those who have shed the blood of the just. (The Christians compared his destruction in the water to Pharaoh's drowning in the Red Sea.)

"Felix, Earl of Wurtemburg, was a great persecutor of the saints, and did swear that ere he died he would ride up to the spurs in the blood of the Lutherans: but the very same night wherein he had thus sworn and vowed, he was choked with his own blood.

"The judgments of God were so famous and frequent upon those that did shed the blood of the saints in Bohemia, that it was used as a proverb among the adversaries themselves, That if any man be weary of his life, let him but attempt against the Picardines — so they called the Christians — and he should not live a year to an end.

"Sir Thomas More, once Lord Chancellor of England, was a sworn enemy to the gospel, and persecuted the saints with fire and faggot; and among all his praises he reckons this as the chiefest — that he had been a persecutor of the Lutherans, i.e., the saints. But what became of him? He was first accused of treason, and then condemned, and at last beheaded.

"Judge Morgan was a great persecutor of the people of God; but shortly after he had passed the sentence of condemnation upon that virtuous lady, the Lady Jane Grey, he fell mad, and in his mad raving fits, he would continually cry out, 'Take away the Lady Jane, take away the Lady Jane from me!' and in that horror he ended his wretched life."

The sin of shedding innocent blood is so deep a sin in God's eyes, he has resolved to judge that sin with all the wrath of heaven!

History clearly shows that almighty God has cast down to the depths all nations and individuals who unmercifully spilled the blood of the innocents and the righteous. Indeed, the historian Josephus saw this as the reason behind the destruction of Jerusalem. He wrote that because Israel sinned against God by shedding the blood of just men and innocents within its gates — even in the temple of the Lord — "their sorrowful sighings multiplied, and their weeping daily increased. It was the blood of the just and innocents that turned Jerusalem into ashes."

The godly Puritan minister John Owen wrote that the fires which destroyed London in 1666 were most likely the result of God remembering the awful shedding of innocent blood under Queen Mary. Owen wrote:

"For in four years of her reign there were consumed in the heat of those flames two hundred and seventy-seven persons — viz., five bishops, one-and-twenty ministers, eight gentlemen, eighty-four artificers, one hundred husbandmen, servants, and labourers, six-and-twenty wives, twenty widows, nine virgins, two boys, and two infants. I say, who can tell but that the blood of these precious servants of the Lord hath cried aloud in the ears of the Lord for vengeance against that once glorious, but now desolate city? Men of brutish spirits, and that are skillful to destroy, make no more of shedding the blood of the just, than they do of shedding the blood of a swine; but yet this hideous sin makes so great a noise in the ears of the Lord of hosts, that many times he tells the world by his fiery dispensations that it cannot be purged away but by fire."

France's King Charles IX was one of history's worst shedders of innocent blood. He massacred the Protestants in Paris unmercifully and gloried in actually glutting himself on their blood. In *The History of France* (pages 791-798) we see another picture of how God judges such blood-shedding. This wicked king was overtaken suddenly by a painfully debilitating and tormenting disease. Eventually, he died a horrible death, "with a great effusion of blood issued out of all the passages of his body." He died wallowing in his own blood!

If every drop of blood of every slain innocent has a voice crying out from the ground, how much longer can our just and holy God withhold his wrath and vengeance?

I ask you — how can God bring judgment on all these shedders of innocent blood throughout history — cutting off and casting down all the guilty — and yet not judge America, which has spilled the blood of multiplied millions of innocents? God, have mercy on us!

In the next chapter, we'll examine another flash point of God's judgment: the rise of militant homosexual power.

The Ominous Rise of Militant Homosexual Power

CHAPTER FIVE

I want to tell you about a certain society — one that cast God aside and consequently sunk into a pit of gross darkness. Despising the light, this society became a magnet for every kind of evil spirit. Law and order collapsed; every man was a law unto himself. The entire society was abandoned to the devil, and no moral force remained to hinder its headlong rush into hell. There was no honor, decency or self-respect left among the people, and they had no reverence for life whatso-ever. Justice and kindness faded away, and they were over-come with lust and licentiousness. They sneered at virtue, their consciences seared and calloused. They scoffed at the fear of God and mocked righteousness. They became totally inhospi-table, possessing the heart and indifference of a beast. They had no pity for the poor. All spiritual desire was extinguished, and gross materialism and fleshly lusts became their gods. The people became totally shockproof, so that the vilest, bloodiest crimes were accepted as normal behavior.

I'm actually describing two societies here: Sodom and America! We know of Sodom's terrible end — and scripture shows us that America is fast becoming another Sodom. In ancient Sodom, homosexuals came out of their closets and became activists, casting a demonic spell over an entire generation of men and boys. They grew politically powerful, controlling everything. And Sodom became the world's gay capital — a society so vile, wicked and crazed with violence that its sins thundered throughout the heavens, filling God's holy environment with a hellish cry.

God dispatched two angels to Sodom, and it seemed even they were shocked by the utter degradation and wickedness they saw. This society mocked family values. (How could any society ruled by a militant homosexual spirit not witness the destruction of decent family life?) No visiting male was safe in Sodom. Roving gangs of homosexuals freely cruised the streets and alleys, looking for rape victims. And no one dared stop them — no politician, no police officer, no uprising of enraged parents.

Yet the generation living in Sodom at this time had received a blessing from God: He had delivered them from a bloody war. While Bera was king of Sodom and Birsha was king of Gomorrah, four powerful nations came against them and took the people captive, plundering everything. But God sent Abraham to rescue King Bera and his own nephew Lot, and everything was recovered. Yet even that great deliverance did not change Sodom's wicked ways. The people took God's blessing for granted and didn't give him credit for the victory.

Like Sodom, America has been delivered by God time after time. Yet we have not so much been preserved against judgment as we're being reserved for judgment — if we do not humble ourselves before God! The Lord demonstrated his great mercy toward Sodom just before he destroyed it. And he did the same for our nation while at war in Kuwait and Iraq.

But, like Sodom, America will not change. Militant homosexuality is going to keep advancing unchallenged, and sin will reign.

In Sodom, the roving gay crowd heard that two men were visiting Lot's house. Within hours, they had surrounded the place, trying to knock down the door to gang-rape the visiting angels. So, where was King Bera then? Where were the politicians? Nobody raised a voice against what was happening. It had become a society both intimidated by and given over to homosexuality. So the angels struck these lust-driven men blind — yet in their blindness, they still groped for the door to pursue their raging lusts (see Genesis 19:11).

If angels can weep, those two most certainly wept over the sad sight of these men, made in God's image, who had sunk to the level of groveling beasts. These depraved men were ready to kill in order to satiate their demonic lust. In fact, Lot was so vexed by these men that he told them, "Here are my two daughters. Take them and rape them all night long!" Now, I'm the father of two daughters. And I can't imagine the kind of power such a militant group could have to drive a man to hand over his virgin daughters to a raving mob. But this mob didn't even want the young women — they wanted men!

Scripture says these homosexuals were not an isolated minority, but the majority (see Genesis 19:4, 14). Did God overlook their sins? Did he put off their day of reckoning? How long did God wait, once this raging homosexual spirit became so bold and brazen it would trample what was holy?

The flash point for the judgment of God comes at the very hour a militant homosexual spirit rises up and attacks what is divine and holy.

The two angels sent to Sodom represented God's interests on this earth — that which is of heaven, divine, spiritual, supernatural. Yet the men of that city were so bold, proud and arrogant they attacked the very things representing God's interests, Lot and the two angels. And in the very hour this homosexual spirit in Sodom attacked the house of righteous Lot, God said, "Enough — I will destroy them!" The next morning, while that militant gay society slept off the night's debauchery, fire and brimstone fell on Sodom. David was right in his testimony: "Thou puttest away all the wicked of the earth like dross...thou hast trodden down all [of] them..." (Psalm 119:118-119).

But, you say, this can't happen to us — because Sodom was not like America. Sodom was born heathen and lived and died heathen. Yet America was born Christian — and still remains Christian. Well, let me tell you about another such society — one born of God and the seed of Abraham, a people once entrusted with the covenants and promises of Jehovah God. This story, found in Judges 19, is about the tribe of Benjamin and a little town called Gibeah.

A Levite priest came to Gibeah to take home his concubine, who had run away to her father's home. A man found the Levite camping on the streets late at night, and he begged him to come to his house because the streets were not safe. Unsafe streets in a small town, you might ask? This was a dwelling of Benjamites, children of once-valiant soldiers of the Lord who had marched under Jehovah's banner. This was once a godly place where children frolicked in the streets, and the praises of God were constantly on the lips of its citizens.

But now another spirit had taken control. Gibeah had become the homosexual capital of the Benjamites, a hotbed of homosexual lust. And a foreboding spirit of violence hung over the town. Children no longer played in the streets. God's name was no longer praised but cursed. This society, born in the heart of God and carried for so long in his loving arms, was now ruled by militant Sodomites. And — as happened in Sodom — a homosexual spirit had risen up to challenge what was holy!

"As they were making their hearts merry, behold, the men of the city, certain sons of Belial [the devil], beset the house round about, and beat at the door, and spake to the master of the house, the old man, saying, Bring forth the man that came into thine house, that we may know him" (Judges 19:22). These men were so bold, so fearless of God, they were ready to rape a preacher! Again, that which represented God's interests on earth became a target of vile spirits. It wasn't enough for these men to have the young men and boys in the town; they also had to touch God!

"And the man, the master of the house, went out unto them, and said unto them, Nay, my brethren, nay, I pray you, do not so wickedly; seeing that this man is come into mine house, do not this folly. Behold, here is my daughter a maiden, and his concubine; them I will bring out now, and humble ye them, and do with them what seemeth good unto you: but unto this man do not so vile a thing" (verses 23-24). Like Lot, this man was saying, "Here's my daughter. Take her — abuse her all you like!"

"But the men would not hearken to him: so the man took his concubine, and brought her forth unto them; and they knew her, and abused her all the night until the morning: and when the day began to spring, they let her go. Then came the woman in the dawning of the day, and fell down at the door of the man's house where her lord was, till it was light. And her lord rose up in the morning, and opened the doors of the house, and went out to go his way; and, behold, the woman his concubine was fallen down at the door of the house, and her hands were upon the threshold" (verses 25-27).

The poor woman had probably been scratching half the night to get back into the house before she died from being sodomized. But the man of the house had gone to bed. "And (the Levite) said unto her, Up, and let us be going. But none answered. Then the man took her upon an ass, and the man rose up, and gat him unto his place. And when he was come into his house, he took a knife, and laid hold on his concubine, and divided her, together with her bones, into twelve pieces, and sent her into all the coasts of Israel" (verses 28-29).

This Levite sent a piece of his concubine's body to every tribe of Israel — and it horrified the people. They said, "Never in our history has something happened so low and vile that someone should cut up a body. What would cause someone to do such a horrible thing?" "And it was so, that all that saw it said, There was no such deed done nor seen from the day that the children of Israel came up out of the land of Egypt unto this day: consider of it, take advice, and speak your minds" (verse 30).

Beloved, the carving up of a dead body was horrible enough. But the worst sin of all was that Gibeah had become a homosexual center, and the whole tribe of Benjamin was ready to fight for their right to be militant, cruising homosexuals. They took up arms in defense of what had happened. By their actions, they were saying, "Our brothers had the right to do what they did."

Yet God sent judgment — and in the ensuing battle, 65,100 men were killed (40,000 Israelites and 25,100 Benjamites).

Then the town was burned to the ground, with all of its militant citizens. Gay Gibeah was left in smoldering ashes!

America is worse than Gibeah! Our whole society is sick. Nothing shocks us. We have become desensitized to evil!

I tell you, America has become sick! You can't tell me that God isn't angry, that he's simply overlooking it all. I once received a note from a well-known evangelist that read, "Don't speak against America. Her best days are ahead. God is pleased!" No! That is exactly what the Bible says the false prophets will claim in the last days!

Almost daily, we hear of bloody, senseless mutilations across the nation. Most of New York City does not even shed a tear when the *Daily News* reports:

• "Baby found in plastic bag near Fulton Street in garbage can..."

• "Nineteen-year-old socialite discarded, wrapped in rug — lying on top of garbage pile outside wealthy East Side apartment house..."

• "Police discover parts of four-year-old girl stuffed in suitcase, left in hallway of Bronx apartment house, set on fire..."

How can we not weep when our public schools are turning into disgraceful sex-abuse centers? The *New York Post* reported on March 20: "SCHOOL SEX SHOCKER! Probe finds shocking sex abuse in schools. Millions victimized nationwide. One in five girls abused before age sixteen..." Teachers, custodians, superintendents, security guards — every level is involved in abusing our children. An executive assistant of a Bronx school board lured a thirteen-year-old boy to his apartment to watch porno movies and to seduce him.

And the American Association of School Administrators was shocked to find out that one in seven boys has been abused by school personnel.

Today we see the sad, frightened faces of millions of innocent children who have been raped by men, forced into incest by their own parents, and seduced by teachers, preachers and priests. You can't tell me God is smiling on America! You can't say our holy, just Lord will sit by as millions more of our children are plundered, raped and destroyed.

America has reached the flash point of God's judgment! We are already like all past societies that permitted the rise of a dominant, defiant homosexual spirit. I wonder if angels are already walking our streets, aghast at the speed with which we're racing toward hell. Yet we can rest assured, there is one thing God will not permit. And when it happens, we can know the hour of judgment has come.

God will not allow homosexual spirits to trample his holy name or to touch his anointed — and yet that is happening right now in America!

In Maine, the *Portland Press Herald* (serving a conservative county) ran this story: "Presbyterian Task Force Recommends Ordaining Homosexuals." It said that a study called the Majority Report claims homosexual activity is not a sin; rather, all sex is morally neutral. The report also contained this stand on adolescent sex: "Advocating 'just say no' is not the answer. What we hope to teach young people is to make good choices — that when it's right to say no they will say no, and when it's right to say yes they will say yes." I ask you — when is it ever right for a child to say yes to sex?

In the same newspaper, the Reverend Rose Mary Denmore, a lesbian, says she is angry that homosexual and lesbian ministers are kept from working with children. She says, "Keeping adult homosexuals separate from youngsters who may be homosexuals deprives them of adult confidantes they may need." Do you hear what she is saying? Now homosexuals want access to our children!

It is one thing for homosexuals to come out of the closet and demand equal and special rights...to move into all levels of government and influence the media...to lobby for privileges as married couples and adoptive parents...to gain enough power to insist the Empire State Building be bathed in lavender lights in celebration of Gay Pride Week...and to have New York's mayor lead their parade, dance with them half the night, call them a discriminated minority and equate them with civil rights leaders and Martin Luther King. But it is another thing entirely when that spirit rises up to touch God's interests on this earth. That's when God says, "Enough!" And all through the Bible, that is the moment when God moved.

And now we see the final defaming of Jesus: A theater production is reported to be coming to New York City, depicting Christ as a homosexual who's involved with his own disciples! Is this the last straw?

God won't tolerate the deviant sexual practices of Christians!

I'm going to be very brave in talking about something God has laid on my heart. I want to talk to you about some of the other deviant sexual practices going on in America. I don't mean the acts of homosexuals in Greenwich Village. And I don't mean the lurid sex murders of a Jeffrey Dahmer, who killed and cannibalized some of his homosexual partners. No, these sinners aren't the ones who break God's heart the most; these have always been given over to their sins. Rather, God's heart is grieved over something more evil than that: HE IS GRIEVED OVER THE SUDDEN MORAL BREAKDOWN OF THOSE WHO CALL THEMSELVES CHRISTIANS!

That's right — in millions of Christian homes, so-called normal, godly people sit before cable TV or a VCR and drink in filthy, shameful, R- and X-rated movies. I believe I'm speaking to literally hundreds of thousands of Christians who are involved in such filth. Indeed, the Holy Spirit spoke to my heart that I may be one of the few voices who warns you of the danger you face. I believe I have to take this stand, before it's too late for many!

TV networks and cable companies now compete to bring the vilest, most perverted movies into America's homes. And untold numbers of "believing Christians" are now being affected by watching pornography. Christian couples are being told, "Pornography can't hurt married adults. In fact, it will enhance your marriage. It will bring a new excitement." Some even say these movies serve as a valve to let off sexual energy that otherwise could cause a spouse to turn to someone outside the marriage. No! These lies are being bought by ministers of the gospel!

Every night and day in this nation, Christians who once would not even think such things now indulge in all kinds of kinkiness — sadism, pain games, wild experimentation. They excuse it by misquoting the verse, "...the (marriage) bed (is) undefiled..." (Hebrews 13:4). They twist this to mean, "Anything goes between married people." No — that's a lie from hell! Pornography is not innocent, and sadomasochistic practices lead to demonic manifestations. It is dangerous and destructive. And it opens your home to every kind of demonic attack!

One Pentecostal minister's wife watched in horror as her husband's lust for pornography destroyed his anointing and changed him into a man she didn't know. He started bringing porno videos home and sitting for hours in his study, drinking in one filthy film after another. Soon he turned into a porno addict — and all his relationships began to sour. His wife could see the demonic influences entering his heart.

Eventually, this man insisted that his wife watch the videos with him — and that they introduce those same sexual acts into their marriage. He said if she didn't comply, he'd leave her. She didn't want her marriage to fail — so she watched the movies with him. She told me, "Mr. Wilkerson, at first I was ashamed. But within two or three weeks, an attraction was building in my heart. It was laying hold of me. One time I was watching, and suddenly I realized we had opened ourselves to demonic possession. We were trying to reenact those pornographic scenes from the videos in our lives — and hell was entering our hearts! I knew that the people who perform in those movies are children of the devil — and we were doing the same things that they were! I ran out of the room, fell on my knees and repented — and God changed me. I told my husband I couldn't do it anymore!"

Her husband left her. He resigned from the ministry and gave himself over to despair. He went downward physically and spiritually, and within a year he was a completely different man, given over to the occult. This woman can tell you something of the hellish stronghold pornography can have on a Christian home. Teenagers are going to hell because their parents have corrupted their own minds. Mom and Dad wake up in the morning, their minds replaying scenes of lust...they go through their workday thinking of lust...they sit at the dinner table thinking of it...they go to bed with it on their minds...and now, in Christian homes all across America, filthy scenes are being played out and reenacted that are straight out of hell!

I believe I'm speaking as an oracle of God to many believers who are reading this. This shame has invaded your life and home, and you may be blinded to its power. If it has taken hold of you, it will destroy you — and God will depart from you! You see, when a people who were once "separated unto God" become so deeply corrupted that they become "devoted to shameful lust," God must depart. And he must call for a day of recompense. He would not tolerate such deep corruption in Israel, and he won't tolerate it today. May you cry out to him for deliverance!

If you're reading this right now, and you're involved with pornography in any way, run to God immediately! Fall on your knees, dear brother, sister or pastor — because the devil has your heart, and the Holy Spirit has departed from you. Up to this point, God's Spirit has been the "restrainer" in our society. He has delayed his judgment, because of his tender mercies. But when God departs, his favor and restraining power leave a society — and they'll leave you as well!

Can you imagine how totally given over to sin America will become when the Holy Spirit departs? If we remain so sin-possessed now while he is near, pleading with us to forsake our sin, what will life be like when he leaves? What will happen when the restrainer is gone? How many Christians will be overcomers then?

Beloved, God's awful shaking of the whole earth has already begun. In the next chapter, we'll see how events taking place throughout the world right now have all been prophesied in scripture.

The Prophets Have Warned Us

CHAPTER SIX

The prophet Isaiah gives us an amazing picture of what will happen on the earth "...in the last days..." (Isaiah 2:2). He says that in the period just prior to Jesus' return, our savior will judge the nations: "And he shall judge among the nations..." (verse 4). This judgment will be terrifying! Isaiah describes it this way:

"The lofty looks of man shall be humbled...the Lord of hosts shall be upon [come against] every one that is proud and lofty...and upon every high tower, and upon every fenced wall, and upon all the [trading] ships...and upon all pleasant pictures [things]. And the loftiness of man shall be bowed down, and the haughtiness of men shall be made low...and the idols he shall utterly abolish. And they shall go into the holes of the rocks, and into the caves of the earth, for fear of the Lord... when he ariseth to shake terribly the earth" (verses 11-19).

Isaiah says this holy shaking of the nations will be so terrifying, people will hide in caves and even rocks to try to escape the terror falling all around them. The Hebrew phrase for "shake terribly" here is "a dreadful shaking." Try to imagine the fear that will grip people during this time. Isaiah says they'll be so shaken, they'll cast their "...idols of silver, and...idols of gold, which they made each one for himself to worship, to the moles and to the bats" (verse 20). All the material things that they've trusted in — their "gold and silver" — will be so devalued, it will be tossed aside as worthless. Why? "...for fear of the Lord, and for the glory of his majesty, when he ariseth to shake terribly the earth" (verse 21).

Already we're seeing glimpses of this. In the early 1980s, I predicted that Swiss banks — historically the world's strongest, most reputable financial institutions — would be plagued by a scandal so awful, no one would believe it. Now we've learned these very banks have been storing money the Nazis stole from Jews they murdered during World War II. It's an abominable scandal — shaking the confidence of all who have trusted in these institutions through the years!

The author of Hebrews confirms that a terrible, last-days shaking will take place: "...Yet once more I shake not the earth only, but also heaven" (Hebrews 12:26). God is saying, in other words: "I'm going to shake everything that can be shaken — every institution, everything that humankind trusts in. And after I've finished shaking everything, the only things that will remain are those that can't be shaken!"

What we are about to see will be terrifying — in spite of any prosperity and ease that have come our way in recent years. And right now, we're seeing the beginnings of this final, terrifying shaking of the nations!

It all started in the Pacific Rim in the final months of 1997. As I mentioned previously, bankers from all over the world rushed to South Korea, Indonesia, Malaysia and other nations to pour billions of dollars of investment into them. If you had traveled to any of these nations just a few months before the shaking, you would have seen Mercedes Benzes

zipping along the roads, women parading in fashionable fin-
ery, shiny new factories springing up in prosperous cities.
But overnight, the balloon began to burst — and nobody can
explain what happened. Banks and currency began to fail,
and nothing could stop the bleeding. I wrote that the International Monetary Fund outlined a plan to pour billions into
these nations, yet I believe it has been to little or no avail.
Now all of these prosperous Asian nations are gripped by
terror. A great economic shaking has befallen them!

• In South Korea, almost overnight, the stock market
lost 80 percent of its value. Real estate bottomed out completely. Factories began closing left and right, and the country
is still anticipating millions of unemployed on the streets. Just
a few months ago, South Korea was the world's eleventh
most prosperous nation. But overnight, it has been shaken to
its very foundation.

• In Indonesia, supermarkets were inundated with panic-
stricken people trying to hoard food. Within a matter of weeks,
"luxury flea markets" popped up, with wealthy people auc-
tioning off their expensive cars and fur coats at a fraction of
their worth. Overnight, these high-living people needed petty
cash just to survive. All their paper wealth was gone.

This terrible shaking isn't limited to Asia, however. We're
seeing it happen all over the world:

• A few years ago, we saw the once-great Soviet empire
crumble virtually overnight. That communist nation once had
a dependable economy. It was proud of its powerful armies.
But suddenly, God began to shake everything! The Iron Cur-
tain fell, and the mighty Soviet Union splintered into pieces.
The economy was totally devastated. Their military might was
crushed. Ethnic wars began between its independent states.

God had brought a terrible shaking — and things changed suddenly!

• The former Yugoslavia has been shaken terribly. You probably remember when the Winter Olympics were held in Sarajevo. That picturesque city had beautiful streets, majestic cathedrals, quaint hillside villages. But Sarajevo was thrown into turmoil. Bombs began to fall — and suddenly ruin replaced beauty. This nation was suddenly plagued by one of the bloodiest, most devastating ethnic wars the world has ever seen. Serbs, Croats and Muslims were locked in a deadly conflict, and it devastated the country.

Today, the same terrible cloud that has darkened these nations is hovering over the United States — and I am convinced our shaking has begun! The stock market we thought was so fail-proof and insulated against disaster is going to be shaken as never before. When the market tumbles, observers will say, "It's just another little storm. We'll weather it." No — our economy will be shaken as never before! Think about it: Many of our exports are going to those badly shaken Pacific Rim nations. And already some of our industries have felt the impact!

Yet the pride and arrogance on Wall Street remain. Young brokers who have never known hard times think their prosperity will never end. Many are investing like drunken sailors — unaware that a terrible shaking is about to happen overnight. All our idols of silver and gold — our booming economy, our computer industry, our possessions — will tumble in value. God is going to rise up and shake everything that can be shaken!

Not one stone shall be left upon another!

The Bible proves that just prior to the time God brings sudden judgment on a prosperous nation, many of his own people turn a deaf ear to all prophetic warnings of a great shaking. Why? Simply put, believers enjoy prosperity just as much as the ungodly do! Of course, there's nothing wrong with enjoying the blessings of God. Our Lord is merciful and caring, and he loves to bless those who walk with him. But, like the heathen, God's people can become soft, satisfied, even consumed by their material possessions. The simple fact is, no one wants to end a prosperous lifestyle. Therefore, whenever a message of judgment comes along — one that suggests our lifestyle may be shaken or even permanently changed — we naturally don't want to hear it.

Now, I can understand why the wicked would mock the warnings and prophecies of righteous prophets. They've been blinded by the prince of this world, and they can't possibly understand spiritual things. But when it comes to turning a deaf ear to hard truth, believers often are worse than the wicked! All through the scriptures — and throughout history — God's people have been unwilling to hear or believe that their good life soon could be shaken by God.

In the Old Testament, God instructed the prophet Isaiah to write a prophetic warning and distribute it to Israel. But he warned Isaiah that the people had already become rebellious to all hard truth: "...this is a rebellious children...that will not hear the law of the Lord" (Isaiah 30:9). God was saying, "I'm telling you ahead of time, they won't hear you. They'll close their ears to all you have to say!"

The people did eventually gather to listen to Isaiah proclaim his awful warnings of a shaking. But they quickly wearied of the prophet's message of judgment. They didn't want to hear that their prosperous lifestyle was in jeopardy. And they told him, "...Prophesy not unto us right things, speak unto us smooth things, prophesy deceits...cause the Holy One of Israel to cease from before us" (verses 10-11).

In plain language, they were saying, "Tell us pleasant things — lift our spirits! We don't want to hear any more of this gloom-and-doom talk. Lighten up, Isaiah! Entertain us. Forget about all this 'holiness' stuff you keep harping on, saying, 'Holiness demands this and that.' It's getting on our nerves. We can't handle all this negative preaching. Our God isn't like that!"

The truth is, if you read the book of Isaiah carefully, you'll discover that this prophet, more than any other, proclaims a message of divine mercy and hope. He speaks at great length of God's tenderness and longsuffering toward his people. Indeed, in this very chapter, even while God's people are resisting his warnings, Isaiah says, "Therefore will the Lord wait, that he may be gracious unto you...that he may have mercy upon you...he will be very gracious unto thee at the voice of thy cry; when he shall hear it, he will answer thee" (verses 18-19).

These indulgent, complacent people had been given numerous messages extolling the mercy and longsuffering of their God. But they convinced themselves that God is only about mercy — and that he's not a God of justice, who has to judge sin and wickedness. They weren't willing to listen to any prophetic messages concerning his holiness and judgment!

I fear many Christians today have fallen into this same condition. They love to hear about the Lord's tender mercies, his gracious, forgiving love, his everlasting lovingkindness. Yes, our God is all of these things — and I preach this as strongly as anyone. But whenever I write a prophetic message or book at God's prompting — one that sounds a warn-ing of impending judgment — the most vociferous critics are ministers and Christians! They write in by the dozens, de-manding, "Take me off your mailing list! I don't want to hear any more of your gloom and doom. God is love. I couldn't serve a God like yours — a God of wrath and judgment!"

In my opinion, there are plenty of hirelings in the pulpit today — cowardly shepherds who are glad to give lukewarm Christians what they clamor for. They preach short, upbeat, positive sermons that are non-threatening, with little or no gos-pel or scriptural content. It's all just a feel-good experience for the people — and it's leading them toward destruction!

Tragically, Israel rejected Isaiah's warnings — and God's people ended up totally unprepared for the shaking that came upon them. They fell into ruin and devastation — because up to the last hour before judgment hit, they were feeding on illusions!

When King Ahab of Israel and King Jehoshaphat of Judah were set to go to war against Syria, four hundred feel-good, false prophets predicted success rather than an impending shaking.

As rulers over God's people, Ahab and Jehoshaphat asked the prophets whether they should go to battle against Syria. Some four hundred false prophets assured them, "Go up [to battle]...and prosper: for the Lord shall deliver it into the king's hand" (1 Kings 22:12). But Jehoshaphat was a true man of God — and when he heard these prophecies, he felt a gnawing in his spirit. He declared, "These men preach prosperity and success, and they claim everything is fine. But something in my spirit says they're wrong." Hearing this, Ahab called for the prophet Micaiah, whom he knew to be intimate with God.

Now, the messenger who summoned Micaiah asked the prophet to soften his message. He urged him, "Give the kings a pleasant word, as did the other prophets." "...let thy word, I pray thee, be like the word of one of them, and speak that which is good" (verse 13). But Micaiah had heard a different word from the Lord. He knew a terrible shaking was coming. He also knew that Ahab would die if he went into battle, and that the armies of Israel and Judah would be totally defeated and scattered. So he was not about to give the kings a soft, smooth, "good" word. Instead, he told them: "My word is only that of one against four hundred. But, gentlemen, I'm telling you — if you go to battle, you will die! God is saying there's danger ahead for you. God is going to judge this land!"

Yet Ahab wouldn't listen. And neither did the army of Israel, the four hundred false prophets, or the messenger — all of whom were living in the land of promise. None of them wanted to hear the truth. Instead, they preferred an illusion of victory and prosperity. Yes, they all knew Micaiah to be holy — but they shut out his message anyway. And Ahab and Israel walked blindly into destruction. The great shaking did happen, just as prophesied!

Amos warned of a shaking.

The prophet Amos also was given a message of warning for Israel — but he came with a message of mercy first. He knew Israel was at the very door of judgment — and so he preached, "Thus saith the Lord...Seek ye me, and ye shall live...Seek the Lord...lest he break out like fire in the house of Joseph, and devour it, and there be none to quench it..." (Amos 5:4-6). He was saying, "If you'll repent — if you'll turn to the Lord and seek him with all your heart — he will be merciful to you. When you cry out, he'll hear you and deliver you. He wants to show you his mercy!" Yet Amos then gave this dire warning: "The virgin of Israel is fallen; she shall no more rise: she is forsaken upon her land...(ye) shall surely go into captivity..." (verses 2, 5).

Did prosperous Israel repent at any of these warnings? No — they rejected Amos' words completely! And they hated the prophet for delivering them: "They hate him that rebuketh in the gate, and they abhor him that speaketh uprightly" (verse 10). When God's true prophets raise their voices to speak hard truth, they become the most hated people of all!

Amos then cried out, "Woe to them that are at ease in Zion...that put far away the evil day...that lie upon beds of ivory, and stretch themselves upon their couches, and eat the lambs out of the flock...that chant to the sound of the viol...that drink wine in bowls, and anoint themselves with the chief ointments [perfume]: but they are not grieved for the affliction of Joseph" (6:1-6). The prophet told Israel, in essence, "You're taking it easy, living in luxury. And you've lost your burden for the poor. You won't believe that your lifestyle will be shaken and disturbed. Now God's shaking has come!"

What a vivid picture of the present-day, backslidden church in America. Couch-potato Christians today don't grieve over our nation's sins. They don't weep over the iniquity in our society. The sad truth is, they don't have time to hear any messages of judgment. They're too busy grabbing their colas and potato chips and settling in to watch sports on TV all weekend!

Amos could hardly believe the spiritual blindness of God's people. To them, life had become one big banquet of good food, good wine and good music. They didn't want to hear a prophet crying out warnings that their party was about to end. So they ate, sang, danced and enjoyed their prosperity. Yet all that time, Amos stood at the gate of the temple, crying, "Wailing shall be in all streets...and in all vineyards shall be wailing...now shall they go captive with the first that go captive, and the banquet of them that stretched themselves shall be removed" (5:16-17, 6:7). "...I [God] will not again pass by [spare] them any more" (7:8).

History shows that Israel didn't heed the warnings of Amos — or any of the other prophets, for that matter. So God "...turn[ed] their feasts into mourning, and all their songs into lamentation...and I will bring up sackcloth upon all loins...and I will make...the end thereof as a bitter day" (8:10). Beloved, it all happened just as Amos prophesied. It is now written down in the history books!

In the New Testament we read that even Jesus' disciples chafed at the hard, nearly unbelievable prophecies of Christ.

In Matthew 23, Jesus predicted the shaking and destruction of Jerusalem. Our Lord saw the apostasy and wickedness of both the priesthood and prosperous Israel. And so, with his disciples standing nearby, he addressed all the people who had crowded into the temple: "...upon you (will) come all the righteous blood shed upon the earth, from the blood of righteous Abel unto the blood of Zacharias son of Barachias, whom ye slew...Behold, your house is left unto you desolate" (Matthew 23:35, 38).

Jesus' disciples were incredulous. He had prophesied all of these awful warnings in the temple — the holy center of their whole society! Quickly, they took their master aside and led him to a vantage point high above the city — and there they pointed out to him everything he'd said would be destroyed: "...his disiciples came to him for to shew him the buildings of the temple" (24:1). Before their eyes was a glorious, magnificent temple, 589 years old. The historian Josephus writes that Herod had just spent eight years and used 10,000 laborers in restoring its greatness. Surely the disciples found it hard to imagine such beautiful antiquity would come to an end. How could all this magnificence be shaken until desolate? After all, prosperous Jerusalem's walls were high, thick, impregnable!

These sincere men must have thought, "If only he would look at the pomp, the stateliness, the greatness of these buildings, he would see how impossible it is for all this to be destroyed." And at that point, they might have said to him, "Master, look at how fantastic all this is. People from all over the world come to Jerusalem. Yet you say it's all coming down — it's all going to be shaken, ruined. How could this be?"

Jesus knew what was on their minds. They were probably hoping he would soften his warnings. But instead, Jesus did just the opposite. After surveying the city calmly, he turned to his disciples and said, "...See ye not all these things? Verily I say unto you, There shall not be left here one stone upon another, that shall not be thrown down" (verse 2).

Beloved, American Christians today are accustomed to even greater prosperity! When we look at our nation — and New York City in particular — we see skyscrapers, magnificent buildings, the center of world commerce, endless wealth and prosperity. (One New York City newspaper reported that a certain apartment in Trump Tower rents for $100,000 per month — and that many others go for $25,000 a month.) We see Wall Street, with its booming world markets and a multi-billion-dollar economy. There can be no question in anyone's mind: We're the richest nation on earth!

As we consider all these things, we think it's absolutely impossible that judgment could be at the door. We simply can't conceive of everything being shaken. Who would believe that one day soon these expensive apartments will lie empty...that people will wander aimlessly in the streets, bankrupt and confused...that multimillionaires will become penniless over-night, their mansions repossessed, their $200,000 automobiles auctioned off at a fraction of their cost...that a thousand fires will burn throughout the city at one time? I ask you — what person living in America today would believe all this? It sounds as preposterous as Jesus telling his disciples, "Do you see all these magnificent buildings? Very soon, not one of them will be left standing!"

The fact is, forty years after Jesus' ascension into heaven, the Roman emperor Vespasian sent his son Titus with an army to besiege Jerusalem. According to the historians Josephus and Eusebius, on August 10, 71 A.D., Titus captured Jerusalem — and a holocaust followed. Titus actually tried to stop his troops from burning down the temple, but he was too late. A mad spirit overtook them, and they torched it, burning it to the ground. When the smoke cleared, not a single stone remained upon another. The Lord's prophecy of judgment was fulfilled to the letter!

We've seen in this chapter how God's prophecies of judgment played out biblically. Now, we'll look at some examples from history of how such prophecies have been fulfilled.

Historical Warnings: The Destruction of London

God instructed Jeremiah to warn wicked Israel, saying: "But go ye now unto my place which was in Shiloh, where I set my name at the first, and see what I did to it for the wickedness of my people Israel" (Jeremiah 7:12). The Lord was saying, "Jeremiah, tell these people to look back into their history and consider my house in Shiloh. Look at the judgment I inflicted on those people because of their wickedness. Consider the great downfall of that house and all of Israel!"

Shiloh was the tabernacle where Eli was the high priest. It was also the place where God wrote "Ichabod" above the door — meaning, "The glory of the Lord has departed." Eli dropped dead, his two sons were murdered, Israel's armies were decimated, and the nation fell into ruin and devastation soon afterward. And now the Lord was saying to Israel, "...because ye have done all these works, saith the Lord...therefore will I do unto this house...as I have done to Shiloh" (verses 13-14).

At the time Jeremiah was given this message of warning, the people of Israel had become cruel, hateful, oppressive. They were murderers, adulterers, blasphemers — yet they still went regularly to the temple to worship and pray. You see, they had invented a doctrine of ease — one that said God was all mercy, and they could do whatever they pleased. In essence, they were saying, "God has released us to do these abominations!"

So Jeremiah stood at the gate of the temple crying out, "Repent! Don't cross the line, but amend your ways! The Lord says if you turn from your sin, he will have mercy. But if you will not hear him — if you continue to trust in lies, commit adultery, swear, and tell yourselves, 'We are free to commit abominations' — he will bring his swift judgment! Go back in history to Shiloh. See how the Lord removed his protective covering from his people. Everything was brought to devastation. And now God is warning you that the same judgment is about to fall on you — because you have sinned just as they did!"

But Israel didn't listen. They conveniently shut out all of Jeremiah's warnings. And God's judgment fell swiftly and severely!

We today do not have to go as far back as Shiloh — because we need only to look back to London, England, of the seventeenth century.

There is an instructive lesson to us in what God brought down on London in 1665-66. At that time, London was the world's most prosperous city. It was known as the "Jewel of the British Empire." The empire itself was so vast, with colonies and lands worldwide, it was said the sun never set upon it. Anywhere you went in the world, at any time, the sun was shining on some territory owned by the British.

London was also known as the business mart of the world. Its ships sailed the oceans, bringing home the wealth of all nations. Moreover, London was filled with stately churches, magnificent public buildings, kings' palaces, great monuments. And it was considered a Christian city, a center for religious activities. A number of great men of God preached in London at the time, and the city was populated by many praying believers.

But London's wealth and prosperity began to corrupt its multitudes. There was a high rate of employment, an abundance of wealth and the finest of materials and goods. And soon people began to indulge their fleshly lusts, wallowing in drinking and feasting. Atheism and agnosticism became acceptable and even popular philosophies of life. Fornication became commonplace, and prostitution grew rampant. Large areas of the city became impoverished, and the poor were neglected and despised.

Many Christians were grieved as this spirit of iniquity fell over London. Great men of God — preachers such as Richard Baxter and John Owen — cried out warnings from the scriptures: "I spake unto thee in thy prosperity; but thou saidst, I will not hear..." (Jeremiah 22:21). These men delivered dire messages to the English population that were so powerful, I shudder as I read them today. They warned of coming judgments, pestilences, the collapse of businesses, fires falling on the city. Some of their messages were so scathing, so piercing, I could never imagine preaching them!

Yet their warnings fell on deaf ears. London simply refused to hear. The people said, "How can the most prosperous city on earth suddenly fall to devastation, fire, pestilence?" But in 1665, a plague of small pox suddenly engulfed London. In just a few months, thousands of people died. The stench of death quickly filled the city, and those who could fled to safer places. Bodies were piled on wooden carts and the poor were buried in mass graves. The pestilence had come as prophesied!

Finally, near the end of that year, the plague was stayed. As 1666 dawned, the crisis seemed to have passed. Yet, did London sit up and take notice? Did the people see God's hand of warning in it all? No! The city immediately reverted to its wicked ways. Now everyone thought they could survive any crisis. London was impregnable, infallible — and their prosperity would last forever! According to English records, the city was 2,770 years old at the time. So some people reasoned, "Jerusalem stood 1,179 years. But we've survived a thousand years longer. How can a city that has existed almost 3,000 years be destroyed?"

Then, on Sunday, September 2, 1666 — at 2 a.m., while London slept — a madman named Hubert set fire to a house on Pudding Lane. Within hours, the fire spread uncontrollably. There had been no rain in London for weeks, and the houses and buildings went up like dry tinder. The night became a blaze of fire and smoke, and people ran through the streets screaming in terror.

There are several written accounts of this infamous burning of the city of London. These accounts describe a raging fire no one could extinguish, spreading throughout the city and consuming everything in four days of sheer holocaust. Eighty-four churches were burned to the ground. Monuments melted down to nothing. Mansions were decimated. Thousands upon thousands of buildings were laid to waste. The city's whole infrastructure was destroyed.

Overnight, the wealthy became paupers. During the fire, they had run into the streets with their precious possessions, yelling, "Forty pounds for a cart!" They were offering what amounted to several hundred dollars just to be able to haul their valuables to safety. But it was to no avail — they escaped only with their lives! Their fine art, expensive jewelry, estate papers, furs, clothes, silverware, crystal — all were destroyed. Here is a firsthand account by a writer of that time:

"Oh, the sad looks, the pale cheeks, the weeping eyes, the smiting of breasts, the wringing of hands that was to be seen in every street and on every corner. What a consternation did my eyes behold upon the minds of all men in that day of the Lord's wrath! There is no expressing of the sighs, the tears, the fears, the frights, and the amazement of the citizens, who were now compassed about with flames of fire. Many rich men, that had enough time to have removed their goods, their wares, flattered themselves that the fires would not reach their habitations. They thought they were safe and secure. But they did not escape."

John Owen, the Puritan, wrote:

"Ah, London, London! How long has the Lord been striving with thee by his Spirit, by his word, by his messengers, by his mercies, and by lesser judgments, and yet thou hast been incorrigible, incurable, and irrecoverable under all! God looked that the agues, fevers, small pox, strange sicknesses, want of trade, and poverty that was coming on like an armed man upon thee, with all the lesser fires that have been kindled in the midst of thee, should have awakened thee to repentance; and yet under all, how proud, how stout, how hard, how obdurate hast thou been!

"God looked that the bloody sword that the nations round

hath drawn against thee should have humbled thee, and brought thee to his foot: and yet thou hast rejected the remedy of thy recovery. God looked that the raging, devouring pestilence [small pox] that in 1665 destroyed so many ten thousands of thy inhabitants should have astonished thee, and have been as a prodigy unto thee, to have affrighted thee but of thy sins, and to have turned thee to the Most High:

"But yet after so stupendous and amazing judgments, thou wast hardened in thy sins, and refusedst to return. By all these divers kinds of judgments, how little did God prevail with thy magistracy, ministry, or commonality to break off their sins, to repent, and to abhor themselves in dust and ashes! Hath not God spent all his rods in vain upon thee?...

"When after the raging pestilence men returned to the city, and to their estates and trades...they returned also to their old sins; and as many followed the world more greedily than ever, so many followed their lusts, their sinful courses, more violently than ever; and this has ushered in thy desolation, O London!...How many within and without thy walls did make their belly their god, their kitchen their religion, their dresser their altar, and their cook their minister, whose whole felicity did lie in eating and drinking, whose bodies were as sponges, and whose throats were as open sepulchres to take in all precious liquors, and whose bellies were as graves to bury all God's creatures in!"

After the burning of London, the knight Sir Edward Turner gave a speech to the king at the convening of Parliament. He said: "We must forever with humility acknowledge the justice of God in punishing this whole nation by the late dreadful conflagration of London. We know they were not the greatest sinners on whom the tower of Siloam fell and doubtless all our sins did contribute to the filling up of that measure, which being full, drew down the wrath of God upon that city..."

The king responded to Turner's speech with a repentant attitude:

"His majesty therefore, out of a deep and pious sense of what himself and all his people now suffer, and with a religious care to prevent what may yet be feared, unless it shall please Almighty God to turn away his anger from us, doth hereby publish and declare his royal will and pleasure, that Wednesday, being the tenth of October next ensuing, shall be set apart, and kept, and observed by all his majesty's subjects of England and Wales...as a day of solemn fasting and humiliation, to implore the mercies of God, that it would please him to pardon the crying sins of this nation, those especially which have drawn down this last and heavy judgment upon us, and to remove from us all other his judgments which our sins have deserved, and which we now either feel or fear...

"Not only the blessed Scriptures, but also king and Parliament, do roundly conclude that it was for our sins, our manifold iniquities, our crying sins, that God has sent this heavy judgment upon us."

London was slowly rebuilt. But it never regained its glory as the center of international commerce!

New York City is the world trade mart today!

Today, American Christians have as our examples of judgment Shiloh, Rome, Carthage, Nineveh, London. Each of these great cities was brought down in righteous judgment — yet they sinned less than our great American cities. Seventeenth-century London had no printed pornography, no X-rated movies, no internet sex, no vile TV, no militant gay organizations. It had no laws against religion, no banning of public prayers, no government-supported abortions.

There is not a doubt in my mind — New York City, Wall Street and the United States are now living on borrowed time. It isn't midnight in America anymore — it's past midnight! From what I read in scripture, God may move in judgment any day now. Maybe some madman or unheeded warning will start the panic that sets everything off. In the coming days we may see the appearance of greater prosperity — but, eventually, the fire of God's wrath awaits us! Even the awful plague of AIDS did not wake us up. Now we are about to come under even more severe judgments!

You might ask, "Brother Dave, why do we need to know all of this now? Can't we just wait to see if all this comes to pass? Why stir us up about something so frightful? Can't we wait till the time comes, and simply ask God to give us all the grace we need then?"

Let me ask you: Why did Jesus go into such great detail in Matthew 24, sparing no words in describing to his disciples what was coming? If you think my warnings are harsh, listen to what our Lord said: "There will be famine, pestilence, earthquakes. You'll face false prophets, deceptions, great tribulations such as the world has never seen. Satan will try to deceive even the elect. And because iniquity will abound, the love of many will grow cold. You will be hated by all. And you'll be delivered up, afflicted — even killed!" (see Matthew 24).

Beloved, Jesus' words here are much stronger than anything you'll hear from any preacher in America today. They certainly weren't what his disciples wanted to hear. So, why did Jesus speak such fearsome, detailed warnings to his followers? He spoke them for one reason alone — to prepare their hearts! He wanted them to be in a state of readiness — to be weaned from the spirit of the age, and to be alert to his coming judgment!

Jesus warned them: "Be ye also ready: for in such an hour as ye think not the Son of man cometh. Who then is a faithful and wise servant, whom his lord hath made ruler over his household, to give them meat in due season? Blessed is that servant, whom his lord when he cometh shall find so doing. Verily I say unto you, That he shall make him ruler over all his goods.

"But and if that evil servant shall say in his heart, My lord delayeth his coming; and shall begin to smite his fellowservants, and to eat and drink with the drunken; the lord of that servant shall come in a day when he looketh not for him, and in an hour that he is not aware of, and shall cut him asunder, and appoint him his portion with the hypocrites: there shall be weeping and gnashing of teeth" (Matthew 24:44-51).

Christ is saying, "On the day of the coming judgment, I don't want you to be revealed as hypocrites or phonies. I want you to be aware — watching, praying, fasting. I want you to be ready at any moment, so that you're not taken unaware. And now I'm warning you ahead of time — my judgment is about to come!"

Forty years passed before Jesus' prophecy to his disciples was fulfilled. Likewise, I'm not saying all these things coming upon America will happen tomorrow or this year. But I do know that very soon everything that can be shaken will be shaken. And this message is all about getting ready, preparing, staying awake.

Beloved, don't be revealed as a phony when the trumpet sounds! Don't just sleep until that time comes. Be a seeker after God's heart — and be in obedience to his word when he returns. Get anchored in Christ now — not in your own righteousness, but in the righteousness of Jesus, by faith. Strengthen your faith in his word, and feed your soul on his promises. Then, no matter what happens, you will be prepared.

In the next chapter, we'll look at how some of God's people were not prepared for judgment — because they misread the times.

isreading the Times

If we want to know what's coming in the days ahead for America, we first must look back. That is, we need to search Bible history to discover how God has dealt with all other nations. By his own admission, God never changes; he is the same yesterday, today and forever (see Hebrews 13:8). James writes that in him there is "...no variableness, neither shadow of turning" (James 1:17). Therefore, we can know precisely how God will act in all his judgments.

I've known devoted Christians who fasted and prayed for weeks, hoping to receive a prophetic word concerning their times. Many believers did this just a few years ago, when America stood on the brink of war with Iraq. The whole world was asking, "What's going to happen? Will God judge us through this? Who can tell us what God has in mind?"

Some of these believers had in mind the Old Testament prophet Daniel, who fasted and prayed regularly and received revelation from the Lord. Yet, the truth is, when Daniel wanted to know what lay just ahead, he looked back into Bible history. He studied the books of Moses — Genesis, Exodus, Leviticus, Numbers, Deuteronomy, focusing especially on Leviticus 26 and Deuteronomy 28. And he studied the writings of the prophets, especially Jeremiah and Zephaniah, who prophesied just prior to Daniel's time.

Now, Daniel didn't always understand everything he read. He even said some of the prophets' meaning was "sealed up until the latter days." But when Daniel needed to know something from the Lord about his present day, he could gain a clear understanding from God's written word. He didn't have to hear the voice of an angel, or receive a divine voice, or fast and pray for days on end. Instead, he testified, "...I Daniel understood by books the number of the years, whereof the word of the Lord came to Jeremiah the prophet, that he would accomplish seventy years in the desolations of Jerusalem" (Daniel 9:2). Daniel was able to read the times accurately by simply studying the revealed word of God. It was through the scriptures that he learned the nature of God and his patterns of dealing with nations.

Before January 6, 1991 — just before the outbreak of the Gulf War — there were many prophetic voices speaking throughout the land. And most of these voices were conflicting. One TV evangelist said God had told him peace was coming, and that President Bush would emerge as a hero and be reelected easily in the upcoming election. Another self-proclaimed prophet told me, "God gave me two words — 'walla' and something else. I don't know what the second word is." I asked him, "Well, what does 'walla' mean?" He answered, "I don't know. Maybe it's a code word for a secret weapon. It could mean something about germ warfare or even a hydrogen outburst." I know this man, and I know he loves God and is sincere in his faith. Yet the word "walla" doesn't tell me anything about how God works. The Bible, however, does!

Many people today have given themselves the title of prophet. They think every word that pops into their minds comes directly from heaven. But Daniel gained prophetic understanding by becoming a student of God's word. He was willing to go to the scriptures and to Israel's history to study how God dealt with his people. And it was only after such deep study of biblical history that Daniel was given a telling revelation. Suddenly he saw clearly why God had judged Israel and allowed them to remain in bondage. They fit perfectly the picture of judgment outlined in Leviticus 26 and Deuteronomy 28!

After discovering this, Daniel said, "...I set my face unto the Lord God, to seek by prayer and supplications, with fasting, and sackcloth, and ashes: and I prayed unto the Lord my God, and made my confession..." (verses 3-4). What was Daniel confessing here? He was saying, "We have not obeyed the word of the Lord, which he set before us by his servants the prophets!" "...therefore the curse is poured upon us, and the oath that is written in the law of Moses the servant of God, because we have sinned against him" (verse 11). Daniel had pinpointed the curses of judgment in Leviticus and Deuteronomy, and declared to Israel, "We're in bondage now because we've sinned against the Lord!"

Beloved, if we want to know what God is saying to us in our time, his word is readily available to us — but, like Daniel, we've got to be willing to dig it out. I believe God wants to speak to us about our present time from several passages in Kings, Chronicles and Jeremiah. These passages not only will help us learn from the past but, moreover, they'll teach us how not to misread our own times.

Tragically, throughout history people have misread their times in several ways. I want to discuss some of the ways we can misread our times:

Leaders of nations misread the times when there is peace and prosperity in the land.

When Daniel studied the behavior of God's people and their leaders prior to Israel's downfall, he was shocked by how badly everyone misread the times. They totally miscalculated everything! Israel thought God was with them — and so they swallowed the false teaching of the peace-and-prosperity prophets who were prevalent in that day. These men declared, "Our bondage will end in two years' time. Then we'll spring back, stronger than ever. We're about to enter a time of great prosperity!" But as Daniel read the writings of Jeremiah, he saw the prophet saying, "No — it's going to be seventy years. You'd better prepare yourselves for a very long bondage!"

Daniel must have thought, "How could these people misread their times so badly? How could they be so blind? They thought they were about to be blessed. But the truth was, God was angry with them. He was preparing to bring war and destruction upon Israel! Yet the people refused Jeremiah's warnings — all the while thinking prosperity was just ahead for them. They didn't know they were going to endure a long period of great suffering!"

Jeremiah had preached to this sinful society from Deuteronomy 28, listing all the curses that would fall on them as the result of God's impending judgment. Yet all the Israelites could see was God's blessings surrounding them. Prior to their captivity, in their good times, they answered the prophet, "Jeremiah — are you blind? Take a look around you. How can we be under a curse of judgment when we've never been so blessed in our lives? If this is the curse Moses talked about, then give us more of it!

"You're totally wrong about that curse in Deuteronomy. You need to go back and study it for yourself. The curse says, 'Cursed shall you be in your cities.' Well, our cities may have a few problems — but for the most part they're all prospering. We're building, planting, buying and selling. All of Israel's city dwellers are happy — making money, getting married, buying houses. The future looks bright!

"The curse also says, 'Cursed shall be your basket and storehouse.' But, Jeremiah, our markets are bursting with goods! Consider all the busy merchants. Their camels and donkeys are laden down with the products of our international trade. There are no shortages, no hard times. We sell products to the whole world. God has to be with us — because Moses said he would bless us on all sides, loading our storehouses. And that's just what he's done for us. We're enjoying the blessings of God!

"The curse says, 'Cursed shall be the increase of your livelihood — your cattle, sheep and livestock.' Well, look around, Jeremiah — there's no way we're under a curse. We have so many animals that if we were to try to sell them all, the market would be depressed. Some curse this is. We've got more cattle than we know what to do with!

"And what about all your talk of the curse of consumption, pestilence, sickness, plagues? Sure, there are a few troubling diseases around. But they're mostly among the poor and the strangers in the land. The rest of us enjoy healthy lives. We're able to work, and we're prospering. Where is any evidence of that curse?

"And how can you say the land is 'turning to iron'? Where are the droughts and the big famines? Name just one acre where the earth is turning to powder. We're getting so much rain now that some places are actually flooding. There isn't any drought here. Our weather is the very opposite of what you're saying.

"Where is the 'smiting of blindness' you keep talking about? Where's the panic? Where are all those people you said would be 'weeping and groping at noonday'? Our synagogues are filled with happy people, Jeremiah. Have you no eyes to see? None of your woes are coming to pass. The people are dancing and celebrating because they're optimistic, hopeful. Unlike you, they believe in this godly nation!"

In America today, we have the same philosophy that the Israelites did!

Right now, many church leaders are saying, "America is still the most blessed nation on earth. If you doubt that, just look at the millions who are fleeing their own countries to try to immigrate here. They're flocking here because we have the world's highest standard of living. We've had years of uninterrupted prosperity!

"In the past two decades, wages have more than tripled. And we're able to feed the whole world. In fact, our granaries are literally overflowing. We have to plow under crops and kill cattle just to keep up the prices, because we can't sell all the food we produce. Leviticus 26 talks about these specific blessings. It says, 'Your threshing shall reach unto the vintage.' Well, who but the United States does that describe? Our harvest has reached its vintage!

"America has been most fruitful, multiplying our population year after year. And we've lived safely in this land. We've never once been invaded by a foreign enemy. The world is afraid of us, because our military is so mighty. Don't you see God's hand in all of this? These are all blessings the Bible tells us about!"

No! We have misread all our years of peace and prosperity, just as Israel did! The apostle Paul writes, "Despisest thou the riches of his goodness and forbearance and long-suffering; not knowing that the goodness of God leadeth thee to repentance?" (Romans 2:4). All of these blessings have been poured out on us so we might repent! God is saying, "I determined to judge you long ago — but then I decided to give you one more chance. So I've poured out my blessings on you, prospering you, giving you peace and security, believing my goodness would lead you to turn to me. But you have not heeded!"

Just before the Great Depression of the 1930s, America went through a period called the "roaring twenties." It was a loud, sensuous, wicked time in our nation, when people wined and dined profligately, bought fur coats in excess, and spent the modern equivalent of $200,000 on automobiles. America's leaders assured everyone our future was going to be glorious. They said, "We see fifty years of prosperity ahead — with two chickens in every pot, and two cars in every garage!" But overnight, the dream ended. Everything crumbled into dust. Why? We misread the times! We said, "God must be with us, because we're blessed and prosperous." But America's boom days ended suddenly. And, beloved, today we are misreading our times of blessing as well!

Likewise, the false prophets in Israel boasted that greater revival, blessing and prosperity were ahead. In short, they said the nation was destined for greatness. But Jeremiah read something else into the times. While these men were prophesying falsely, this righteous man's heart was breaking:

"My bowels, my bowels! I am pained at my very heart; my heart maketh a noise in me; I cannot hold my peace, because thou hast heard, O my soul, the sound of the trumpet, the alarm of war. Destruction upon destruction is cried; for the whole land is spoiled: suddenly are my tents spoiled, and my curtains in a moment. How long shall I see the standard, and hear the sound of the trumpet? For my people is foolish, they have not known me; they are sottish children, and they have none understanding: they are wise to do evil, but to do good they have no knowledge" (Jeremiah 4:19-22).

Jeremiah knew history! He had studied God's laws in Leviticus and the words of the previous prophets. And he understood from all these books what was about to happen in his generation. So, this man could stand up and cry boldly, "You may see prosperity — but I see a backslidden people. I see a generation headed into imminent disaster!"

God's people misread the times during superficial revivals.

Israel experienced a superficial revival after enduring one of the worst periods in its history. During that dark period, Manasseh ruled Israel — and he was later declared the most wicked king in the nation's entire history: "...Manasseh seduced them to do more evil than did the nations whom the Lord destroyed before the children of Israel" (2 Kings 21:9). Israel's evil was even worse than that of the heathen nations surrounding them!

Indeed, Manasseh did more to bring down God's anger and wrath on Israel than any other king: "Moreover Manasseh shed innocent blood very much, till he had filled Jerusalem from one end to another...provok(ing God) to anger..." (verses

16, 15). God said, "...Behold, I am bringing such evil upon Jerusalem and Judah, that whosoever heareth of it, both his ears shall tingle...and I will wipe out Jerusalem as a man wipeth a dish, wiping it, and turning it upside down" (verses 12-13). God was saying, "I've had enough!" Jerusalem was headed for judgment because of Manasseh's evil.

But something happened just before judgment struck. God raised up a righteous man and a holy remnant in Jerusalem: King Josiah and his court. I referred to this in a previous chapter — but now I want you to extract some deeper truths about his reign. Josiah inherited the throne as a child, but the scriptures say he did right in the eyes of the Lord: "...(Josiah) walked in all the way of David his father..." (22:2). This young man looked at the evil all around him and decided to begin a purge. He started in Jerusalem, then cleaned up Judah, Israel and even parts of Samaria. He burned down all the idolatrous temples Solomon had built on the mount of abominations, where for years they had stood as an unholy "embassy row." He hewed down the houses of prostitution and sodomy, and slew all the temple prostitutes. He destroyed the occult shrines and killed the occult priests and priestesses. And he broke all the idols into pieces and burned human bones on the shrines' altars, signifying they were desecrated forever.

Then Josiah restored the house of God itself. He repaired the altar and reinstituted temple worship according to God's design. And he called upon the nation's judges to judge righteously, warning he would deal severely with anyone who accepted bribes. And, finally, he sent out godly teachers to call the people back to the God of their fathers.

Up to that time, Josiah didn't have God's word for guidance. He had only the Spirit of God to lead him. Then, after his great reformation in Israel's laws and government had taken place, Josiah discovered God's written word. The scriptures had been lying dormant for years in the temple, gathering dust. But one day a priest found them — and he brought them to Josiah and read them aloud.

After Josiah heard God's holy word being read, he fell on his face in anguish: "And it came to pass, when the king had heard the words of the law, that he rent his clothes. And the king commanded Hilkiah...saying, Go, enquire of the Lord for me, and for them that are left in Israel and in Judah, concering the words of the book that is found: for great is the wrath of the Lord that is poured out upon us, because our fathers have not kept the word of the Lord, to do after all that is written in this book" (2 Chronicles 34:19-21). This godly king cried, "Woe to us! Everything I've heard from God's words of judgment describes us. We're candidates for the curse!"

What were the words Josiah heard? First, he heard Moses' command to Israel, laid out plainly in Deuteronomy: "Ye shall walk after the Lord your God, and fear him, and keep his commandments, and obey his voice, and ye shall serve him, and cleave unto him" (Deuteronomy 13:4). Josiah also heard Jeremiah's prophecy: "...(Israel has) a whore's forehead, thou refusedst to be ashamed" (Jeremiah 3:3). "...Judah hath not turned unto me with her whole heart, but feignedly, saith the Lord" (verse 10). God was saying, "You're faking your repentance. You're only halfhearted about it. You still haven't turned to me!"

Josiah's heart was smitten when he heard these prophetic words. Israel was in the midst of one of the greatest reformations in its history — yet little of it had touched the people's hearts! Josiah saw that it didn't matter whether he cleaned up the nation outwardly and legislated holiness. If the people didn't repent in their hearts, the curse of Deuteronomy would fall upon them. Now the king cried, "I've purged the land, breaking down all idols, enforcing order and instituting godliness. And outwardly the people have responded. But, according to Jeremiah, true holiness isn't taking hold in their hearts. Their repentance is all on the surface — there's no depth to it. And if that's true, then all this has been in vain!"

Right now, the church of Jesus Christ seems to be calling for the same kind of reformation Josiah started. We want our leaders — the President, the Congress, our entire government — to call America back to God. We want them to thwart the rising political and social power of radical homosexuals, to legislate against the bloodshed of abortion, to outlaw pornography and gambling, to bring God back into our schools and courts, and to purge America of its murder, drugs and senseless violence.

Yet, suppose our government does all these things. Suppose it passes such laws of godliness — and suddenly America possesses a form of godliness. Suppose the land is purged of casinos and porn shops, the murder rate is reduced, abortion is no longer allowed, homosexuals aren't granted special privileges, and the Ten Commandments are allowed back into our courtrooms, schools and prisons. I ask you — would that stop the judgment of God? No! Unless there is an awakening of the heart — unless Americans call upon God because we're convicted of grieving him by our wickedness — our judgment will merely be delayed!

You may wonder, "How shallow can a revival be?" Jeremiah writes: "Run ye to and fro through the streets of Jerusalem, and see now, and know, and seek in the broad places thereof, if ye can find a man, if there be any that executeth judgment, that seeketh the truth; and I will pardon it. And though they say, The Lord liveth; surely they swear falsely. O Lord, are not thine eyes upon the truth? Thou hast stricken them, but they have not grieved; thou hast consumed them, but they have refused to receive correction: they have made their faces harder than a rock; they have refused to return. Therefore I said, Surely these are poor; they are foolish: for they know not the way of the Lord, nor the judgment of their God" (Jeremiah 5:1-4).

Jeremiah was saying, in essence, "You're misreading the times! You're saying, 'We can't be under judgment. We're a godly nation.' But judgment is about to strike!"

Many Christians today are misreading God's time for their own lives!

Some believers today think they have plenty of time to get right with God — and so they cling to a besetting sin. Yet, when God's fist of judgment strikes, shaking the whole world by sudden events, these believers will be caught unaware. They'll be sleeping in the arms of some secret lust — and even the worst judgments won't be able to move them! Their hearts will have become so hardened, they won't be stirred by any kind of judgment, no matter how severe. They'll die clinging to a fleshly habit God told them to give up long ago!

Others misread the time they have left to make restitution. These believers are in no hurry to reconcile themselves to their estranged brothers and sisters before Jesus comes. Indeed, some Christians still carry grudges after many years — even at this hour of judgment: "Therefore if thou bring thy gift to the altar, and there rememberedst that thy brother hath ought against thee; leave there thy gift before the altar, and go thy way; first be reconciled to thy brother, and then come and offer thy gift" (Matthew 5:23-24). "If ye forgive men their trespasses, your heavenly Father will also forgive you: But if ye forgive not men their trespasses, neither will your Father forgive your trespasses" (6:14-15).

God brings quick, decisive judgment on all unforgiving people. So, be sure you don't misread the signs in your life! Today, God may be speaking into your life with his goodness — but tomorrow, judgment could strike. You may think, "Everything's going okay" — but soon you'll see trouble like you've never seen it before. You'll see a withering in your life, your home, your work. And no amount of fasting, praying or sacrificing can change it. Until you make things right with your brothers and sisters, you're misreading the times!

God wants us to know that we can have his perfect peace, no matter what the future holds. In the next chapter, we'll learn how we can have and keep his perfect peace.

erfect Peace in a Time of Panic

I've spoken throughout this book of the terrible financial panic that's soon going to fall upon America. Yet, at this point, I have to let you know — God has provided a way for all of his children to have perfect peace in that time of panic!

Recently, I spent some time rereading several of the prophetic messages I wrote earlier in this decade — especially some messages from 1990 and 1991, just a few years after the "October Crash" on Wall Street. At the time, New York City was teetering on the brink of a severe financial shakeup. Unemployment was skyrocketing. The stock market was on a downhill slide. Real estate was dead, with virtually no building or construction taking place. In lower Manhattan, commonly known as the downtown business district, 40 percent of all office space was vacant. Economic fear spread throughout the city.

As I reread one particular message from that time — entitled "The Desolation of America" — I was startled at what I'd written. In that message, I said that the worst thing God could do to America would be to send a huge wave of prosperity upon us. If he did this, we could know he was sending a final mercy call to our nation — just before bringing down judgment!

That's just what is happening in our nation right now. Yet, let me state to you again very clearly: I don't know when all the turmoil I've written about in this book is going to take place. In fact, at times I've thought, "I've written about God's coming judgment for years now. The Lord has been laying this message on my heart over quite a long period of time — and yet none of it has come to pass!" Recently, however, as I reread the chapters in this book, an urgency came over my spirit. And now I believe that very soon — possibly even within the next few years — we're going to see the beginnings of the terrible shaking God is about to bring upon our economy. Specifically, here is what will happen:

The stock market is going to crash, and the bond market will experience a meltdown. As this upheaval hits, many large corporate investors will probably pull out in time; they always seem to know how to escape such crises. (This is just what happened in the days before the Great Depression, which was set off by the crash in 1929. Many wealthy businessmen saw what was coming and cashed out of the market. Then later, when everything became cheap, they bought up properties and investments with their available cash.)

On the other hand, when the coming crash hits, it's going to wreak terrible havoc on individual investors. Indeed, these common people will be the ones who suffer most during the hard times. Today, 45 million American families own some share of the bull market. They've gambled on the stock market through their computers and the internet, investing some $2 to $3 trillion. And when the crash comes, their paper profits will disappear within days!

Not long ago, a leading government official warned small investors against such gambling on the stock market. He stated, "People are leveraging their houses, getting 110 to 125 percent mortgages on their homes, and using the cash to try to strike it rich — all because there's been an upswing in the market, and nobody wants to be left out." It's true — in the first few months of 1998, there was an increase of 15 percent or so in the stock market, especially in the top 100 stocks — and individual investors began trying to capitalize on that. But this official warned very bluntly, "We're headed toward troubled waters, and you've leveraged all you own. You're going to lose your investments, your homes, everything!"

Please understand — the coming crash won't just be some temporary lull in the market. It may appear to some observers that such a crash can be avoided. But this time around, there won't be a sustained rally of any kind. Simply put, the American economy is about to be struck by the fist of almighty God!

Millions of Americans have shut their eyes to the blatant immorality taking place in Washington, D.C.

A frightening attitude toward morality has been adopted by most Americans — including many Christians! Some 75 to 80 percent of Americans polled have declared in so many words to the world, "It doesn't matter what our President, congressman or any other leader does immorally. Let them all fornicate, indulge their lusts, commit perjury and cover up their sins as they please. Morals just don't count in America anymore. The only thing that matters is whether we prosper. As long as we have a booming economy, none of the rest of those things matters!"

The prophet Jeremiah describes this attitude in very sober terms: "...they overpass [overlook] the deeds of the wicked...yet they prosper..." (Jeremiah 5:28). Right now, I believe God is responding to this evil mentality in America, saying, "So that's your attitude? Well, if your morals are so mixed up that you care more about the almighty dollar more than about righteousness, I'll fix things very quickly!"

The fact is, God alone controls the economies of this world. Contrary to all modern thinking, our financial well-being isn't ruled by the wisdom of humans. Only the Lord, who upholds all of creation by the word of his mouth, determines the destinies of nations — economic and otherwise! And he commands: "Thou shalt remember the Lord thy God: for it is he that giveth thee power to get wealth..." (Deuteronomy 8:18).

The Lord warned Israel against the proud, arrogant boasting of all who thought they prospered because of human skill and ability: "(If) thou say in thine heart, My power and the might of mine hand hath gotten me this wealth...it shall be, if thou do at all forget the Lord thy God...I testify against you this day that ye shall surely perish...as the nations which the Lord destroyeth before your face, so shall ye perish..." (verses 17-20).

The word "perish" here means "to be broken and undone, to lose it all." This doesn't refer merely to being crushed with debt — but to being completely undone, ruined! God was telling Israel, "If you think for one moment that these material blessings have come to you because of your own skill and efforts — if you take all the credit for them, and refuse to acknowledge me — I'll take them all away! Consider all the nations before you, who thought they were blessed by their own doing. You're going to end up as they did — losing everything!"

Right now, Wall Street has completely abandoned God in its clamor for the almighty dollar. Think about it for a moment: When has any leader of a financial institution given God even an ounce of credit for the prosperity our nation is enjoying? On the contrary, the big moneymakers and analysts in America have mocked God and pushed him out of sight. When did anyone cry, "Thank God, we're being blessed and prospered," as the stock market first broke 7,000 and then 8,000 and continued to go upward? And when the closing bell rang on those days, did anyone on the trading floor say, "God has allowed us to accumulate all this wealth"? No! He is rarely acknowledged in even the smallest way — not even with a single prayer of gratitude. Instead, the cry has been, "We're invincible! Our power, might and skill have brought us these riches."

Americans today think there will be no end to their prosperity.

One financial expert has stated outright, "We've become the smartest and most skilled financial nation on the face of the earth." Yet, Japan made the same claim ten years ago — and within one year their entire real-estate market collapsed! Recently, the president of Sony warned that Japan was headed for a full-blown depression. He compared the country's prime minister to U.S. President Herbert Hoover, who told Americans just before the Great Depression hit that our nation was going to prosper.

Both scripture and history make it perfectly clear: No

power, might, skill or knowledge of humankind ever gained any nation the wealth it accumulated. Yet, amazingly, as America has grown ever richer, we've completely forgotten God in the process. If you believe the Bible is God's word, and that he's true to his word, then you must believe America is going to see its wealth perish and evaporate, just as Moses prophesied. The Lord has said, "You're not giving me credit for all the blessings I've given you! Instead, gold and silver have become your gods. Not only have you insulted me by refusing to acknowledge me as the source of all your wealth — but now you've pushed me out of your society. If you don't see that I've been merciful to you — that I'm the one who has enabled you to have all these blessings — then get ready to face the worst financial panic you've ever known!"

Even with all the storm clouds gathering, most moneymakers still haven't allowed God to enter into their thinking. Not long ago, the *New York Times* ran a photo of young Wall Street businessmen lighting cigars with twenty-dollar bills. The accompanying article was about all the successful people who are flaunting the wealth they've accumulated. They spend $5,000 for a bottle of wine. And they buy $100 cigars but smoke only half of them before throwing them away.

As I see these things happening in our society, I know that every passing day brings us closer to the fulfillment of Moses' prophecy. Like all past nations who refused to acknowledge the Lord, we're going to be humbled. God's word clearly tells us a panic is coming. And the word "panic" is defined as "a sudden, overwhelming fear that spreads quickly and produces hysteria." Soon, God will merely speak a word — and a sudden hurricane of confusion will hit the American economy!

The biblical prophets have said that in such times, the wicked will cry for help and wail over their great losses. But right now, the only sound that can be heard among the wicked in America is boasting. The prophet Isaiah writes, "...the wind shall carry them all away; vanity shall take them..." (Isaiah 57:13). In other words, pride, arrogance, greed and covetousness will all be swept away by the great winds of adversity. Then Isaiah adds, "When thou criest, let thy companies deliver thee..." (same verse). This means, "Let your gathering of advisers and experts get you out of your trouble! They told you the economy wouldn't falter. They assured you all was well, that the sky was the limit. So, now let them tell you what to do. Let all your prognosticators, those who read the stars and tell you there's no end in sight, advise you how to escape the calamity!"

I believe God is going to do two significant things in the coming panic — and these two things are already happening in our midst:

1. God is going to take away all peace from the wicked.

"There is no peace, saith the Lord, unto the wicked" (Isaiah 48:22). There is a false peace common to all workers of wickedness — a peace that's based not on reality but on a lie. And right now, that false peace has fallen over Wall Street and the financial markets — indeed, over all of America!

Moses spoke of those who would reject God's frightful warnings. He said such people would turn a deaf ear to God's prophets, and instead the spiritually blind would "...bless himself in his heart, saying, I shall have peace, though I walk in the imagination of mine heart, to add drunkenness to thirst" (Deuteronomy 29:19). Right now, this describes everyone who's outside the church of Jesus Christ. A majority of Americans are now looking out for number one, building their own nest egg. And even though these unbelievers can see what's looming ahead, they're looking to make one final killing, so they can stash enough away to ride out the coming storm.

As I've driven through the affluent towns of suburban New Jersey, I've seen the million-dollar estates of young businessmen who gamble everything they have on the stock market, mortgaging themselves to the hilt. Here is their motto: "It's okay if a crash hits. After all, if I go down, my neighbor will too. We'll all go down together — because we're all in the same boat!"

Beloved, these are the people Moses was referring to — people who have "blessed themselves" with false security. Not only are they thirsting for wealth and prosperity, but they've become drunken with it — stupefied by it all! They've developed a mentality that says, "I don't want just a little drop — I want the whole thing. I want to make it big!"

Moses clearly warns against such arrogance: "The Lord will not spare him, but then the anger of the Lord and his jealousy shall smoke against that man, and all the curses that are written in this book shall lie upon him, and the Lord shall blot out his name from under heaven" (verse 20). Likewise, Isaiah writes that when God begins to judge such people for their wickedness, the first thing they'll experience is a total loss of peace: "The way of peace they knew not; and there is no judgment in their goings: they have made them crooked paths: whosoever goeth therein shall not know peace" (Isaiah 59:8).

Isaiah describes the turmoil that these wicked people will face: "The wicked are like the troubled sea, when it cannot rest, whose waters cast up mire and dirt. There is no peace, saith my God, to the wicked" (57:20-21). Right now, the sea appears to be calm; there's clear sailing ahead, with only a few waves here and there. But just wait! Soon the storm will hit, the sea will begin to boil and the waters will be troubled. So, you ask, what is this troubled sea that cannot rest? It's the entire population of those who've turned from God and now face his anger as he fulfills his word of judgment! Such people may have a false peace right now, but it won't last. An inner gnawing has begun in them — because God is already taking away their peace! Material things cannot satisfy the inner gnawing for reality.

I ask you — how much longer do you think God will allow us to thumb our noses at him? How much longer will he let us refuse to blush at the most violent sins this nation has ever seen? How much longer will he put up with all the wickedness in America, before he says, "Enough!" Right now our nation is like the nation of Israel as described by Jeremiah: "...their houses [are] full of deceit: therefore they are become great, and waxen rich. They are waxen fat, they shine...Shall I not visit for these things? saith the Lord: shall not my soul be avenged on such a nation as this?" (Jeremiah 5:27-29). God himself is saying, "How can I not bring judgment upon such flaunted sin and compromise?"

You might be tempted to say, "It's plain to see why God sent his judgment on Israel and other past societies in the Old Testament — but America is different!"

You may think, "God has to spare us. After all, he's called us to evangelize the world." Actually, most of our churches' missions programs are dying. Think about it: Wouldn't it be unjust of God to judge the wickedness of his own chosen people — or to destroy Nineveh, or to take down Rome — and yet spare America? Our sins are far more evil than those societies' ever were. And our cup of iniquity is still overflowing!

If God is holy and just, no respecter of persons, then he must say to us the same thing he said to wicked Israel: "I will surely consume them, saith the Lord: there shall be no grapes on the vine, nor figs on the fig tree, and the leaf shall fade; and the things that I have given them shall pass away from them" (8:13). God is saying, "I'll cause their good times to fade away. I'll dry up all their riches and make their prosperity wither. In my great mercy, I gave them all this wealth — all the things they now lust after with covetous hearts. In spite of all my blessings, they rejected me — and now I'm going to take it all away!"

All the multiplied thousands who've had no time for God — who've laughed at moral standards and made wealth their idol, who've leveraged their homes to raise more money to gamble with stocks — are going to lose their savings, their homes, their fine cars and furniture. Many will try to declare bankruptcy. Indeed, this is happening already, even in these so-called good times, before the real panic comes. Last year alone, 1.3 million individual Americans declared bankruptcy. And soon there will be such a glut of people filing for bankruptcy, the federal government will have to pass legislation to stop the financial hemorrhaging.

I believe that in the not-too-distant future, almost every block on America's streets will be lined with "For Sale" signs in front of homes. There will be sellers only, and very few buyers. The housing market will collapse — and we could witness in our nation what happened in Japan, Indonesia and other nations of the Pacific Rim. There may be a 70 to 80 percent devaluation in real estate — and a rush to liquidate everything to raise cash. Just as happened in Indonesia, we'll see used $100,000 Mercedes Benz cars selling for less than $20,000. Banks and mortgage companies will be stuck with billions of dollars' worth of property they can't unload. As Jeremiah prophesies, "Their houses shall be turned unto others..." (6:12).

And there will be mass unemployment. The *New York Times* recently ran a photo of the masses of unemployed workers in South Korea. Not long ago, that nation had almost no unemployment — and now it is on the brink of a depression. Whenever employers advertise for a single position, thousands of applicants show up. Likewise, when the crash hits in America, we'll see endless unemployment lines on our streets.

Incredible financial upheaval is now plaguing Japan. Recently, a scandal broke out in that nation's central banking system. Within weeks, the system's president and seven other high-ranking officials committed suicide. And soon in the United States, when the financial panic strikes, the hysteria will be worse than anything our nation has ever seen. Many common people will take their lives, because they'll be unable to cope with the collapse of their personal finances. All across the nation, the suicide rate will leap dramatically.

As I read Jeremiah's prophecies today, I find that his words to Israel apply totally to America. He writes: "The spoilers are come upon all high places through the wilderness: for the sword of the Lord shall devour from the one end of the land even to the other end of the land: no flesh shall have peace. They have sown wheat, but shall reap thorns: they have put themselves to pain, but shall not profit: and they shall be ashamed of your revenues because of the fierce anger of the Lord" (12:12-13). He's saying, "Shame upon your prosperity and profits! When judgment falls upon you, you'll be filled with woe, because you'll lose everything. No flesh will have peace in that day of reckoning!"

This is all just one side of the coin. I mentioned previously that there are two things I see God doing in America before and during the coming panic. Here is the second thing I see him doing:

2. In the coming panic, God's trusting people will be blessed with perfect peace.

The Lord declares, "I create the fruit of the lips; Peace, peace to him that is far off, and to him that is near, saith the Lord; and I will heal him" (Isaiah 57:19). The Hebrew word for "peace" here is "perfect peace."

I believe that as we're surrounded by chaos and hysteria in the coming days, America is going to witness the greatest testimony to God's glory and power it has ever seen. How? All of America will see that many of God's people possess his perfect peace! In that time the Lord is going to raise up a people who've been endowed with his absolute, perfect peace — the peace that Christ himself now enjoys at the right hand of the father. And we're going to live, move and breathe in that wonderful peace.

Scripture says God will keep all who trust him "...in perfect peace, whose mind is stayed on thee: because he trusteth in thee" (26:3). And right now, many of God's people are making this commitment to him: "I'm going to set my heart to seek God through everything, no matter what comes. I'm going to give him all that I have and all that I am. I believe his judgment is coming — so I'm going to prepare myself for him, as his bride!"

God first made his promise of perfect peace to those in Judah who were undergoing a great chastening of the Lord upon their land. God was bringing down all the high fortresses and walls, all the pomp and riches people leaned on, "...even to the dust" (25:12). Even the faithful remnant who still trusted in God were shaken to their very core. Yet during that time, God told Isaiah to reassure these faithful believers: "The Lord is going to keep you in perfect peace — if you'll simply trust him!" The prophet said, "Lord, thou wilt ordain peace for us..." (26:12). In other words: "God is going to set up in our hearts his very own peace. He wants to give us a peace that can't be shaken!"

Likewise today, when panic strikes in America — when the ominous news begins to send shock waves of fear across the land, and hysteria mounts — God's people won't be able to avoid feeling the huge wave of human anxiety. That's right — I will feel it, you will feel it, all Christians are going to feel it. Such feelings are inevitable; it's simply human to have this kind of reaction to such terrible chaos. Yet, at the same time, God will put within us the resources needed to take immediate control of every fearful thought and bring it into obedience to the truth of Christ. And his Spirit will fill our very beings with his perfect peace!

God is going to act quickly to devastate America's economy — not only as judgment upon the sins of this nation, but for another reason as well.

The upheaval that's coming to America is not meant as judgment on the church — but as a purging of the church! Indeed, to those who love Christ and cling to him, the coming holocaust won't be judgment at all. You see, although God comes to the wicked as an avenger, he comes to the righteous as a redeemer!

Now, the bride of Christ consists of righteous believers from every tribe, tongue and nation on the face of the earth. And God's word tells us that we are all to be espoused to Christ as his bride-in-waiting. Scripture also tells us the Lord chastens all of his children, whom he loves. And right now, God is chastening his bride in order to purge her — because he sees she's become spotted by the spirit of the age. Greed, materialism and covetousness have crept into his church. And God's response is, "If I wait much longer, my beloved bride will be inundated. I simply will not give over my bride to the wicked one. I won't let her be swept away by love of material things."

God's greater purpose in breaking down the American money machine is to deliver his redeemed children from the contagious spirit of materialism and worldly-mindedness now engulfing our nation. Think about it: Unless you work for a church or ministry, every bit of talk you hear on your job is probably about money, pleasure, possessions. God is never given even a passing remark, except as a curse. Your co-workers constantly focus on their new clothes, their upcoming vacation, their shrewd investments, their latest raise, their next car. And all their worldly talk is contagious. It can't help but vex your spirit, just as Lot's soul was vexed by living in wicked Sodom!

Tragically, many Christians today are chasing the almighty dollar, trying to strike it rich, just like the rest of the world.

At one time these believers were conscientious about keeping their white robe spotless in preparation for meeting their Lord. They adored him, studied his word and sought him diligently. But now the spirit of greed and covetousness has laid hold of their hearts, and they indulge in filth just like the rest of our godless society. So God has finally stepped in and said, "No — I won't let the enemy have you!"

I believe that this, more than anything else, is God's motivation for moving in judgment against our nation. Scripture says he is coming for a bride without spot or wrinkle: "That he might present it to himself a glorious church, not having spot, or wrinkle, or any such thing; but that it should be holy and without blemish" (Ephesians 5:27). The fact is, everything God does on this earth, he does with his bride in mind. All of his dealings with us have one purpose behind them: "How will this affect my chosen ones — my children, my church, my bride?"

Today God sees prosperity and abundance pulling his bride away from him. She's growing more and more earthbound — richer, more comfortable, less mindful of Christ. And now the Lord must move quickly to wean her back to himself. How will he do this? First, he'll remove everything that has preoccupied her time and attention. He declares, "All of this wealth may have been a blessing to my bride at one time. But now there's so much garbage in my church, the only way to get her clean is to rid her of all these worldly possessions!"

As we read the history of God's people in the Old Testament, we see a pattern repeated over and over. God blessed and prospered his people...they grew wealthy and full of possessions...and then they forgot their Lord, lightly esteeming the one who made all their blessings possible. Scripture says: "Jeshurun waxed fat, and kicked: thou art waxen fat, thou art grown thick, thou art covered with fatness; then he forsook God which made him, and lightly esteemed the Rock of his salvation" (Deuteronomy 32:15). The people grew fat on their wealth and eventually forgot the source of it all. And so it is in America today!

In the coming panic — when you see the stock market crashing and behold the hysteria that grips our nation — you can be sure it's much more than just a payday for our godlessness and immorality. If you're a true child of God, you must see it primarily as his wake-up call to his bride! He's calling us out from this worldly system and preparing us for a complete return to him. His Spirit is now crying out, "Come out of Babylon! Don't be a partaker of her filth, covetousness and sins. Cling to me once more!"

In Isaiah 59, the prophet lists all the reasons why God must send judgment: hands defiled with blood, lying lips, feet that run to do evil, imaginations full of wild and evil thoughts, mischief, violence, iniquity, crookedness, spiritual blindness, departure from God. Isaiah says, "According to their deeds, accordingly he will repay, fury to his adversaries, recompence to his enemies..." (Isaiah 59:18). Yet, what is God's primary purpose in repaying wicked nations for their evil deeds? It is that during the time of judgment, "So shall they fear the name of the Lord...and his glory..." (verse 19). God wants us to recognize our evil ways — so that we'll return to him! "The Redeemer shall come to Zion, and unto them that turn from transgression in Jacob, saith the Lord" (verse 20).

I realize the primary focus of Isaiah's prophecy here is on the coming of the Messiah to a spiritual Israel. Yet I believe this passage is also saying God will come to his people with chastening as he sends fury upon his adversaries. And so, today, as our Lord visits Wall Street and Washington, D.C. as an avenger — repaying with judgment all the pride, arrogance, covetousness and godlessness of our nation — at the same time he'll visit his church as a redeemer — awakening his bride, alluring her from the enticements of the world, and preparing her for her final homecoming to him. This won't be judgment on his children, but mercy. It will be his rescue of us from the sinfulness of a godless society!

True Christian values have been corrupted and weakened — and the financial panic that's coming will be God's way of purging those values and restoring godly values in those who love him.

At this time in America's history, many Christians have become liberal and loose in their moral values. They indulge in behavior that just a few years ago would have made them blush. Indeed, who would have believed that the time would come when believers would embrace and condone the homosexual lifestyle...bring pornographic movies into their homes...surf the internet in search of filth...become social drinkers...indulge in fornication and adultery?

Right now, adultery is rampant in Christian circles — including the ministry. And fornication has become commonplace among teenagers — including young Christians. These bewildered young people are having sex at any time, without feeling so much as a pang of guilt. And now, as if rampant sexual sin in the body of Christ weren't bad enough, a group of Christian ministers in California has allowed a witch into its fellowship. She's considered a religious leader — and these pastors are embracing her!

Our values as Christians have rapidly eroded in just the past few years. Christian parents now allow their teenage children to do as they please, with no real guidelines for godly living. In the spirit of "political correctness," the older generation simply doesn't want to offend their children — and so the young people make a pastime of fooling their mothers and fathers. Many parents are just lazy; they set their children in front of a TV and let it do their babysitting. Yet these days, many of Disney's shows are full of greed, sex, even witchcraft — and they're filling our young people's minds with evil!

I believe the coming financial crisis is going to be the best thing God could do to save the youth of America. He's going to take his young loved ones to "school," where they'll learn how to get along with less. He'll make them say goodbye to $150 sneakers, credit cards and shopping sprees, new cars and expense accounts, expensive clothes and entertainment systems. Indeed, the young people who know the fear of God will receive a great education from their Lord during these hard times. They'll learn that wealth is fleeting: "...riches certainly make themselves wings; they fly away as an eagle toward heaven" (Proverbs 23:5). They'll emerge with a strong work ethic and godly values. The coming upheaval is going to straighten out the perverted values in all believers — both young and old!

What does all of this have to do with perfect peace for true believers?

We are told not to despise "...the chastening of the Lord, nor faint when thou art rebuked of him" (Hebrews 12:5). In other words, we are not to question God — not to murmur or complain — because while he is judging the wicked, he'll also be lovingly chastening his church. "For whom the Lord loveth he chasteneth, and scourgeth every son whom he receiveth" (verse 6). To "scourge" means "to lay the rod on the back, or to spank." God is going to apply his rod to all of our compromises, worldly-mindedness, foolishness and evil desires. "If ye endure chastening, God dealeth with you as with sons; for what son is he whom the father chasteneth not?" (verse 7).

Everyone in the body of Christ is going to feel the Lord's rod of correction during the coming hard times. It will be the working of his perfect will to bring his church back to holiness. And as we understand that he is lovingly at work in us, his perfect peace will fill our souls — and we'll experience a supernatural calm and rest. Indeed, scripture says that all who are willing to learn by the Lord's chastening will enter into this perfect peace: "No chastening for the present seemeth to be joyous, but grievous: nevertheless afterward it yieldeth the peaceable fruit of righteousness unto them which are exercised thereby" (verse 11).

Beloved, the coming time of chastening is going to bear much holy fruit in us — all for the Lord's greater glory. You see, when awful storms of chaos are breaking out all around, God will have a people whose "habitations are peaceable" — whose hearts will not fail them for fear as they see all that's coming upon the nation. They will enjoy a calm, quiet rest — rejoicing in the salvation of their God!

The Lord gave the captive Jews in Babylon a glorious promise — and this promise applies to every child of his today: "I know the thoughts that I think toward you, saith the Lord, thoughts of peace, and not of evil, to give you an expected end. Then shall ye call upon me, and ye shall go and pray unto me, and I will hearken unto you. And ye shall seek me, and find me, when ye shall search for me with all your heart" (Jeremiah 29:11-13). The phrase "to give you an expected end" here means, "to give you hope for the future."

Yes, dear saint, we're going to suffer — but through it all, God has laid out a future for us. His chastening won't feel good — but it will lead us closer and closer to our bridegroom, who awaits us at the final wedding, where we'll be joined with him forever.

The Lord has given us a secret to surviving the coming hard times. And in the next chapter, we'll discover that secret. It is available to every believer!

Knowing God's Voice: The Secret to Surviving the Coming Crash

I have faithfully warned in this book that America is on the brink of a financial holocaust. Our nation is about to come under severe chastening from the Lord, and great changes will take place as a result of the coming economic and social upheavals. Simply put, life as we know it is about to be changed forever. The American dream is about to become the American nightmare!

It's important for you to understand up front that Christians are going to suffer these unprecedented troubles and hardships just like everyone else. The fact is, when God's judgments fall upon a nation, everyone suffers. We see a clear example of this in Jesus' lifetime. Christ forewarned the inhabitants of Jerusalem that their city soon would be besieged by enemy armies and utterly destroyed. He advised them, "When you see those armies approaching, flee to the mountains!" The historian Josephus writes that years later, when Titus led his Chaldean divisions toward Jerusalem, the majority of believers in Jerusalem did flee. And so they were delivered during that awful time of destruction, because they received the word of direction their Lord had given them. Yet they experienced deprivation in their fleeing to mountains, caves and neighboring nations.

The author of Hebrews speaks of a certain group of Christians who lost everything and became homeless. Incredibly, he says, these believers "...took joyfully the spoiling of (their) goods..." (Hebrews 10:34). And in the very next chapter, he describes such faithful believers as "...wander(ing) about in sheepskins and goatskins; being destitute, afflicted, tormented ...they wandered in deserts, and in mountains, and in dens and caves of the earth" (11:37-38).

These verses disprove the false doctrine that says Christians will escape the dark times ahead, remaining untouched by all the fearful things that are about to come upon America. Such teaching is absurd and unscriptural. Yet, right now, some false prophets are teaching that a select group of Christians will have a kind of "super faith" that will protect them from all pain, suffering and testing!

This is just the kind of heresy that shipwrecked the faith of scores of Christians during the Boxer Rebellion in China. The Chinese converts knew an awesome, violent upheaval was coming. But certain missionaries told them Jesus would rapture them away before they had to face any of the coming violence. When the violence hit, and no such rapture occurred, many of those hundreds of thousands of Chinese Christians lost their faith, because they weren't ready to face suffering. They were persecuted — they lost their houses, lands and possessions — and they were beaten, bloodied and killed. Tragically, their leaders hadn't prepared them for what was coming — and the Christians who survived felt lied to, cheated, deceived.

Likewise today, most Christians in America are not prepared to suffer. Many don't believe they have to endure privation and loss, and hope the hard times will last only a short while. Such believers love to hear the words of the false prophets: "Don't worry — good times are just ahead! This difficult period isn't going to last long. It's just a glitch in the economy. There's nothing to fret over!"

These same kinds of heresies were proclaimed in Jeremiah's day as well. Yet Jeremiah knew better than to listen to them. He knew that awesome changes were about to fall upon God's people — the very kinds of upheavals I've been warning about in this book. The Lord was about to move in upon Judah with awesome judgments, and every person would face a sudden, drastic change in lifestyle. The nation would be crushed economically, their times of prosperity would end, the people would be led away captive, and their bondage would not be short-lived. According to Jeremiah, their hard times would last seventy years!

This holy prophet cried out his warnings for thirteen years before the judgments hit with gale force. He went to the temple and the courts, warning the king, the princes, the leaders, the elders — but no one would believe him. False prophets ridiculed his warnings, including Hananiah, who predicted, "Within two full years will I bring again into this place all the vessels of the Lord's house...the...king of Judah, with all the captives of Judah...for I will break the yoke of the king of Babylon" (Jeremiah 28:3-4). Hananiah prophesied that God would crush the Babylonian empire, and Judah would bounce back within two years. But it was all a false prophecy, causing the people to hope in vain. The hard truth was, Judah's difficult times ended up lasting seventy years — just as Jeremiah had prophesied!

You may ask, "How bad can things get when God judges a nation for its transgressions?"

The book of Lamentations is Jeremiah's heart-cry over all the terrible conditions that fell upon Judah after God fulfilled his word of judgment. In this book, the prophet recounts how Jerusalem was besieged and destroyed, the temple was burned to the ground, and the nation fell into utter sorrow and misery. Everywhere he turned, Jeremiah saw images of abject horror that sent him spiraling into despair: Starving mothers boiled their babies just to have food to eat. People who once had lived comfortably now dug through garbage cans, looking for anything edible. The Levites, the priestly lineage of Israel, begged for food. And once-strong, healthy people lay dying in the streets — all because Jerusalem had come under judgment.

These awful sights brought Jeremiah so low, he almost lost his faith. He knew that even though these people were rebellious and full of wickedness, they still were God's children. Yet, the Lord seemed to have no trouble judging them or even burning down his own holy temple. Dismayed by it all, Jeremiah began his lamentation by asking, "How could this be, Lord? How could these woes have befallen your people so quickly? How could such a prosperous society be stricken so suddenly? Your beloved city, Jerusalem, was a jewel in the world's eyes — and now it's in total servitude to heathen enemies. Why didn't they see this coming? Why didn't anybody listen to me?" (see Lamentations 1:1).

If you want to know how quickly a nation can disintegrate under divine judgment — if you want to witness just how bad things can get for such a society — prayerfully study Lamentations 1. You'll see how severely God "...afflict(s)...for a multitude of...transgressions" (verse 5). Beloved, the same kinds of judgments that fell on Judah are about to come upon our nation! As happened in Jerusalem, the coming crisis in America won't be just a small slap on the wrist. It won't be a temporary glitch in the stock market, a short-lived collapse when the market takes a dive for a week or two and then bounces back up. No, the judgments that are about to fall on us are going to be worse than any of us could imagine — and they're going to last a long time!

Many Christians have written or called our ministry's offices, worried about their financial future because of my warnings. They inquire, "Where can I put my money? What investments will be safe during the dark times ahead? Will there be any protective havens for my savings? And what about my Social Security and my retirement funds? Also, what's God saying about debt and mortgages? Will I lose my house in the coming holocaust? What will I do if I lose my job and can't find employment? How will I be able to support my family? Should I store up food? Brother Dave, how can I prepare for such an awful event? If what you say is true, where can I turn for some answers?"

I don't give any financial advice — but I am in touch daily with the world's one and only dependable adviser!

For every question I have on any matter, my trusted adviser has an answer. He's been with our ministry since the very beginning. Eleven years ago, when we moved our offices back to New York City, he moved with us. And he has directed every real estate transaction we've made here: He helped us buy the historic Mark Hellinger Theater on Broadway, where our church holds its worship services at the crossroads of the world. And he secured the Isaiah House where we feed the poor, and the Timothy and Sarah Houses where we minister to addicted men and women.

Yet he's not only our financial and real estate adviser. He's also our attorney, family adviser, counselor and travel guide. Indeed, he guides us in literally everything we do and face. And the last time I talked with him (which was this morning, before I finished this chapter), he assured me he would continue to provide steady guidance for us throughout the coming financial crash. He told me we had absolutely nothing to worry about!

Best of all, my adviser doesn't mind if I call him every day. And it makes no difference to him what time of day I call. Even if I want to talk in the middle of the night, it's no bother to him. In fact, he says, he's delighted whenever I call him, because it shows my clear trust in him. And besides, if I don't come to him, he'll end up knocking on my door, asking me to dine, and wanting to talk about everything I need. He's available to me at all times — even from hour to hour — through any crisis, no matter how long it may last. And he has promised me that no matter how hopeless a crisis may appear, he knows the way through it and has all the resources I might need.

My adviser encourages me, "David, you don't ever have to worry about a thing. I've been through these kinds of things many times before." Indeed, he has specialized in guiding his clients through hard times for centuries. For example — by his wisdom and his words, literally hundreds of thousands of people were sustained for forty years in a drought-stricken, snake-infested wilderness. They survived in a place where there was no food or water, an area totally uninhabited by other human beings. He told them, "Just heed my voice. Take my advice, and do what I tell you. If you listen to me, you'll be blessed — and you'll come out of your hard times stronger than when you entered them."

My adviser also gave this kind of caring, specific guidance to a godly man named Noah. First, he warned Noah that his society was about to fall. He essentially told him, "Noah, I realize that, as things sit right now, catastrophe looks impossible. But look around you at all the building and growth you see going on — all the buying and selling, eating and drinking, marrying and prospering. I tell you, it's all about to end! Everyone thinks the party's going to last forever. But after a generous grace period, it's all going to come down overnight. Noah, I advise you to build an ark to prepare for that time — to save yourself and your family from the coming destruction!"

Then my adviser actually laid out the plans for Noah's ark and gave him all the dimensions in exact detail. He showed him where to put the window, where to put the door, how big to build the ark. And he said, "If you'll just do it my way, you'll survive — you'll make it through the crisis." Then he told Noah how long to preach to his society, with warnings of the coming destruction. And he also instructed Noah in how to collect and preserve a world-class collection of animals — truly a monumental task!

When that society was brought down, Noah and his family were saved from the destruction. How? It all happened by the word of my adviser. He is in the business of keeping and caring for his clients, no matter what crisis they face. Of course, by now you realize my adviser is your adviser as well — the Lord himself! And it's amazing to see how, time after time throughout the Bible, in every kind of crisis, God has always been intimately involved with his people.

The Lord was involved with David, the sweet psalmist, when that man fell upon hard times.

When David returned home with his army to Ziklag, he found his town reduced to ashes by a band of raiders. His home had been leveled, and his family all had been taken captive. There was absolutely nothing left. Everything he'd worked for — all his cattle, his furnishings, his possessions — were gone. As he stood among the rubble, penniless and homeless, he must have been terrified, not knowing if his loved ones were even alive. He had no one to turn to in that moment. In fact, his own soldiers were ready to stone him, because they blamed him for leading them into battle and leaving their loved ones unprotected.

So, David turned to my adviser. Scripture says, "David enquired of the Lord, saying, Shall I pursue after this troop? Shall I overtake them? And he answered him, Pursue: for thou shalt surely overtake them, and without fail recover all" (1 Samuel 30:8). David followed my adviser's counsel — and he did recover all! He was delivered in a time of total, complete devastation. How? His deliverance came through the word of the Lord — detailed instructions that he received personally. God merely spoke his word — "Go, pursue them, and you'll retake everything" — and it all came to pass.

The Lord also provided for his faithful prophet Elijah during a time of devastating privation. Elijah had stood before King Ahab and all of Israel, prophesying that God would judge the nation's wickedness with a long draught. The land wouldn't see even a drop of rain for three years, and the people would face utter devastation: food shortages, a wrecked economy, shrinking herds of cattle, withering crops, starving people.

As Elijah looked ahead to the coming crisis, things must have looked absolutely hopeless to him. But God had a specific survival plan in mind for his faithful servant. "The word of the Lord came unto him, saying, Get thee hence, and turn thee eastward, and hide thyself by the brook Cherith, that is before Jordan. And it shall be, that thou shalt drink of the brook; and I have commanded the ravens to feed thee there" (1 Kings 17:2-4). God was telling Elijah exactly where to go and what to do. He instructed the prophet, "Go east to the Jordan River, and there you'll find a little tributary that runs off, called Cherith. You can get all the drinking water you need from that brook. In addition, I've arranged for food to be delivered to you daily, by my courier ravens!"

I ask you — how could any person, in a million years, ever dream up this kind of plan for survival? How could Elijah ever have imagined he'd be sent to a hidden brook to find water to drink, when there was nothing but drought everywhere else in the land? How could he ever have thought a daily supply of bread would be brought to him by ravenous birds that ate everything they sunk their beaks into?

Later, times got hard for Elijah, because the brook finally dried up. But my adviser stepped in again, giving the prophet another fresh word of direction. He said, "Arise, get thee to Zarephath, which belongeth to Zidon, and dwell there: behold, I have commanded a widow woman there to sustain thee" (verse 9). Again, I have to ask — how could anyone ever think a poor widow, in the midst of a depression, could feed a man for days, weeks, months on end? Elijah must have thought, "This woman has no job, no husband to provide for her, no resources. And we're in the midst of a depression. How could she provide anything, Lord?" But the fact is, God uses the most despised, insignificant things of the world for his glory. And he told Elijah, "If you'll go to her and do what I tell you, you'll survive. Listen to me — heed my direction — and you'll make it through!"

Beloved, the evidence is overwhelming: God — our adviser, counselor and survival expert — has a detailed plan for every one of his children, to help us face the worst of times! We may suffer in the coming days, but our Lord will make sure we won't have to beg for food and that we'll always have a roof over our heads. And even if one part of his survival plan for us appears to begin to fail, he'll continue to direct us faithfully, saying, "Go here, go there..." He'll give us specific, detailed directions by his personal word to us!

Our Lord pledges to be totally involved in the daily care and keeping of all who trust him in times of panic and collapse. He'll speak clearly to every individual who makes up his body, giving specific directions, dimensions, times, places, names, addresses, promises, miracles. He wants us to know, "Your ways are not my ways, and your thoughts are not my thoughts. I have set aside provision for you that you know nothing about!"

When I finished this book and reread it carefully, I felt overwhelmed by it all!

Immediately after rereading all the chapters I've written in this book, I thought, "Oh, Lord — please, don't let this happen! Let it be just a bad dream I've had. Continue your blessings on our nation!" Then, as I spent time in prayer, I realized

I had to hear from God further before delivering this message. I cried out, "Father, I can't publish this, unless you help me understand how you intend to shepherd your flock through this crisis. Please, show me how you're going to sustain your church in such trying times. You must give me a word of hope — a message of encouragement for your people!"

Now, we know from scripture that God takes no pleasure in sending divine judgments to punish wickedness. It's simply libelous for us to say otherwise of our Lord. The Bible says, "For he doth not afflict willingly nor grieve the children of men" (Lamentations 3:33). The literal meaning here is, God does not afflict wicked people "from the heart." Even when he's sending chastening or judgment, he doesn't desire the suffering of his children. On the contrary, it's a hurtful thing to him.

On the other hand, the Bible says, "Wherefore doth a living man complain, a man for the punishment of his sins?" (verse 39). How can any of us murmur when judgment falls on us because of our wickedness? The fact is, God must and will afflict the wicked with "the rod of his wrath" (verse 1). And very soon, the Lord is going to deal with America's wickedness.

Yet I believe my beloved adviser has given me a hopeful word for God's people, to help them face the perilous times ahead. Indeed, he has devised a very simple, uncomplicated plan by which he will protect and keep his people. What is this plan?

God's plan is that we hear his voice daily!

God wants us to know that no matter how difficult things may get for us, he will sustain all who trust in him — by the

131

power of his still, small voice, speaking to our inner man daily.

This is confirmed by the prophet Isaiah: "And thine ears shall hear a word behind thee, saying, This is the way, walk ye in it, when ye turn to the right hand, and when ye turn to the left" (Isaiah 30:21). You have to understand, Isaiah delivered this word to Israel in the very worst of times. The nation was under judgment, in absolute ruin, with everything breaking down. God had given his people "the bread of adversity and the water of affliction." And so Isaiah told Israel's leaders, "Turn to the Lord now! He wants to give you a word of direction — to speak to you, saying, 'Go this way, go that way, here's the way...'" But they wouldn't listen. No one wanted to consult the Lord. Instead, they devised their own plan of survival. They decided they would turn to Egypt to deliver them! They thought they could rely on the Egyptians' chariots, horses and supplies to see them through.

Yet, God did not spend all of his judgment on Israel at that point. Rather, he decided to wait patiently until the bottom fell out of every plan. He said, "While they're running around scheming how to survive, I'll wait. I want to show them my mercy, in spite of their wickedness!" "Therefore will the Lord wait, that he may be gracious unto you...that he may have mercy upon you..." (verse 18). Sure enough, every human-designed plan Israel employed was ruinous. Everything failed, and things only got worse for the nation. Finally, when all their schemes had fallen through, God told the people, "Now, let me take over! Open your ears, and I will speak to you. I know the way out, and I will direct you. I want to guide your every move, to the right and to the left, to deliver you. I'll lead you by my voice — speaking to you, telling you what to do, down to the very last detail!"

Perhaps you don't have to wait for a coming crisis to hit — because you may already be in one of your own. The truth is, it doesn't matter what difficult time you face — whether it's your present financial or family problems, or the hard times just ahead for our nation. What matters — what's vitally important — is that you get to know the voice of God. You'll never survive unless you know and hear his voice through your trial!

God desires that every child of his knows and hears his voice.

Sadly, great numbers of Christians do not know God's voice. Some can go for months, even years, without ever receiving an intimate word from the Lord in their inner man. Oh, God did speak to them at one time. But over the years, they've learned to silence his voice in their hearts. They worship a God whom they never allow to converse with them. They claim to love him — but they never experience a free-flowing communion with their creator. Others have been turned off by so much foolishness among those who believe that every word that pops into their minds is divine. Such people boast, "God told me" — yet the "word" they hear is only their covetous flesh taking voice!

God's word makes it clear how desperate he is to talk with his people. For example, he gathered all of Israel — fathers, mothers, children, grandparents — at the foot of Mount Sinai, and there he made his voice known to them clearly. Later, in the book of Deuteronomy, Moses recounts this scene, saying, "The Lord talked with you face to face in the mount out of the midst of the fire..." (Deuteronomy 5:4). "Out of heaven

he made thee to hear his voice, that he might instruct thee..."
(4:36). God's voice gave them great and detailed plans on how
to survive the wilderness journey, how to maintain their health,
how to devise a portable tabernacle. What a wonderful, mar-
velous thing for Israel. They served a God who spoke to
them! Jehovah was a living God — not like all the dead,
stone idols worshiped by the surrounding heathen nations.
And he spoke to his people personally, clearly, directly. Even
today, the great thrill of any believer ought to be the hearing
of the voice of his shepherd. As John the Baptist said, the
friend of the bridegroom rejoices to hear the bridegroom's
voice.

But, in this instance, the voice of God disturbed Israel
deeply. Something about its very sound bothered them. So
they sent elders and leaders to speak to Moses about it. First,
they said, "...we have heard his voice out of the midst of the
fire: we have seen this day that God doth talk with man, and he
liveth" (5:24). Yet, what these leaders said next seems to make
no sense whatsoever: "Now therefore why should we die?
For this great fire will consume us: if we hear the voice of the
Lord our God any more, then we shall die. For who is there
of all flesh, that hath heard the voice of the living God speaking out of the midst of the fire, as we have, and lived?" (verses
25-26).

These leaders had just confessed they'd heard God's voice
out of the fire and lived. Yet now they were telling Moses,
"(You) go thou near, and hear all that the Lord our God shall
say: and speak thou unto us all that the Lord our God shall
speak unto thee; and we will hear it, and do it" (verse 27). Why
did these people suddenly want a secondhand word from the
Lord? Why didn't they want to hear God speak to them

personally, face to face, as he had before? They should have thrilled to hear their Lord's voice speaking to them. So, what made them shy away from it? There is only one reason:

They knew God's voice would speak to them about their hidden, pet sin of idolatry!

These same Israelites had packed and brought with them into the wilderness thousands of small silver and gold idols from Egypt — pagan good-luck charms. So, while they were giving lip service to worshiping Jehovah God, they were still cleaving to the idols of Egypt. And the Lord's voice had already sounded loud and clear on this subject, in his commandments to them: "Thou shalt have none other gods before me" (verse 7).

In the New Testament, Stephen testifies that those Israelites had offered halfhearted sacrifices in the wilderness for forty years. While they were supposedly serving Jehovah alone, the whole time they "...took up the tabernacle of Moloch, and the star of your god Remphan, figures which ye made to worship them..." (Acts 7:43). Stephen was saying, "The people would give God praise in public — but, secretly, they held onto their idols. They wanted to have something to back them up, just in case he didn't come through for them!"

These Israelites realized that if they drew near to God in intimate conversation, he would point out their hidden idols, giving them no rest. They knew the only things they could bring to him in their prayer closet were guilt, fear and a troubled conscience. So, instead, they decided to rely on a man — Moses — to hear God's voice for them. After all, Moses couldn't see into their hearts and bring conviction, the way the Lord could. They told him, "Go get the word from God and bring it back to us. We'll obey whatever he has to say!"

This is the very reason so many Christians today do not know or hear God's voice: It is by choice! At one time God spoke to them clearly, saying, "Don't do that. It will destroy you! Forsake your secret sin. It will hinder our relationship and cost you abundant life!" But it is precisely because of those warnings that these believers no longer go into their secret closet. They know when they get alone with the Lord and he begins to speak, he'll finger their pet sin. They may tell their pastor, "Preach it! Give me the truth, no matter how red-hot it may be with conviction. I want to hear whatever God's word says to me. I'm ready to live by what you preach, dear shepherd." Yet, the whole time they think, "I'll listen — just as long as it isn't God himself putting his finger on my bosom sin."

The Lord has only one word for such Christians: "You have an idol — now, lay it down! How can I work with you unless we walk in agreement? How can I speak to you, lead you, guide you in hard times, if you've cut off my voice? If you'll simply choose to lay down your idol, my Spirit will give you the power to lay it down. Then you'll be able to hear my voice and obey it — and you'll walk in freedom and abundant life!"

If you want to know and hear God's voice in the days ahead, be ready to have him speak of cleansing before he speaks of direction.

Many Christians want God to tell them how to invest their money, how to hold onto what they've earned, how to provide for their family, how to keep their business or career afloat in difficult times. But the truth is, before God gives us a word of direction in any of these matters, he'll first speak to us about his commandments.

"These things I command you, that ye love one another" (John 15:17). God will first speak to you about your actions at home with your wife and children — about your quick temper, your grudges, your unforgiving spirit, your heart of treachery, your TV-watching habits. He'll point out every hidden, secret thing in your life — and he'll lovingly tell you, "I want to be your adviser, your counselor, your guide, your protector, your provider. I want to walk with you through every trial and hardship. And I want to favor, bless and keep you by my Spirit. But first, you have to get honest with me about the hidden idols in your heart. Right now you're holding onto them — but you must give them up! We simply can't walk together unless we agree on these matters of your heart!"

After Israel's leaders went to Moses with their request, God drew a line. He said to those who no longer wanted to hear his voice: "O that there were such an heart in them, that they would fear me, and keep all my commandments always, that it might be well with them, and with their children for ever!" (Deuteronomy 5:29). And to those with divided hearts, God said: "...Get you into your tents again" (verse 30). In other words: "Do what you want — go on about your business. But now you'll no longer hear my voice personally. You don't want to trust in me. You don't want me to lead or guide you. You've already decided you're not going to lay down your idols. So, go ahead and make your own plans. I'll speak to you now only through others!"

These Israelites wandered in the wilderness for forty years, never hearing a direct word from God. Tragically, they lost touch with him, completely cut off from his voice to them. As you might expect, they lived all those years in fear and dread

— unhappy, miserable, sorrowful, always murmuring and complaining. They constantly fretted and worried about their children, showing no faith in God whatsoever to protect them. They even accused God of bringing them into the wilderness purposely, to make them suffer and kill them off.

But God answered them, "...your little ones, which ye said should be a prey, and your children, which in that day had no knowledge between good and evil, they shall go in thither, and unto them will I give it, and they shall possess it" (1:39). "But as for you [parents], turn you, and take your journey into the wilderness..." (verse 40). In other words: "Your children will survive, because I will deliver them. And they'll thrive in my promised land, which I'll give to them as an inheritance. But as for you — you'll never set foot in that land, because of your stubborn unbelief!"

It is the worst kind of unbelief — indeed, it is an affront to God — to think our Lord would ever abandon your children. God doesn't take kindly to such thinking. His word assures us our small ones are always in his caring hands, safe and protected. And so we must confess the same: "Father, my children are yours. I turn my entire family over to you. Direct us, lead us, guide us!"

During the crisis in Israel, God set Moses apart as an example. The Lord said to him, "But as for thee, stand thou here by me, and I will speak unto thee..." (5:31). He promised Moses he would continue to hear his voice — directly and personally! And he invited Moses to draw near to him and receive all the direction he needed: "Ye shall observe to do therefore as the Lord your God hath commanded you: ye shall not turn aside to the right hand or to the left. Ye shall walk in all the ways which the Lord your God hath commanded you, that ye may live, and that it may be well with you..." (verses 32-33).

Likewise, in the coming crisis in America, God is going to set apart a people who'll be an example to the rest of society. These set-apart ones won't be caught up in the panic. Instead, they'll walk in total peace, because they trust the Lord with their whole being. And they'll hear God speaking to their hearts, "Come to me, all you who love the sound of my voice. Open the door, and enter your secret closet to be with me. Sit before me, and let us sup together. I want to converse with you — to lead you and guide you — to give you my direction!"

Today, you and I are invited to draw near to God, and to ask him for his guiding Holy Spirit — because he promises to give the Spirit to all who ask!

When scripture says the Holy Spirit "abides" in us, it means God's Spirit comes in and possesses our bodies, making it his temple. And because the Holy Spirit knows the mind and voice of the father, he speaks God's thoughts to us: "Howbeit when he, the Spirit of truth, is come, he will guide you into all truth: for he shall not speak of himself; but whatsoever he shall hear, that shall he speak: and he will shew you things to come" (John 16:13). The Holy Spirit is the voice of God in and to us!

If you have the Holy Spirit abiding in you, he will instruct you personally. Please know he doesn't speak only to pastors, prophets and teachers, but to all followers of Jesus. This is evident all through the New Testament, as the Holy Spirit led and guided his people, constantly saying to them, "Go here, go there...enter this town...anoint that person..." The early believers were led everywhere and in everything by the Holy Ghost!

And the Spirit never speaks a single word contrary to the

139

scriptures. Instead, he uses the scriptures to speak clearly to us. He never gives us a "new revelation" apart from God's word. Rather, he focuses on the total revelation we have in Christ. He opens up to us his revealed word, to lead, guide and comfort us, and to show us things to come.

I am convinced God speaks only to those who, like Moses, "come and stand by him." This means we have to spend quality time with the Lord daily — waiting on him to open our hearts fully to hear his voice, not being rushed in his presence, believing he loves to speak to us. He won't keep anything from us — and he'll never allow us to be deceived or left in confusion.

Recently, as I spoke at a ministers' conference, a pastor heard me tell of some of the coming judgments I've mentioned in this book. Afterward, he came to me with a downcast look and said, "Brother Dave, I'm scared. I've just launched a multimillion-dollar building program with my church. If what you're saying is true, then where's that going to leave us? What's going to happen to us now?"

I looked him straight in the eye and said, "If God spoke to you, telling you to do this, then he'll see it through. Leave it in his hands, and don't fret about it. He will provide all. After all, churches were built in the midst of the Great Depression in the 1930s."

Likewise, beloved, if you have a mortgage, trust your heavenly father to provide for it. Yet, even if some financial failure does occur in your life, the Lord will faithfully give you further directions, just as he did for Elijah — explicit, detailed directions for every aspect of life. And the same goes for all of your investments. He will guide you — if you seek him diligently for clear direction. You need no prophet or financial expert. Let God be your broker! You are in good hands with the almighty Lord. He has said, "I haven't given you a spirit of fear, but of power, love and a sound mind" (see 2 Timothy 1:7).

Yes, God is going to purge America, because his holiness demands it. But I don't believe this signals the end of our society. I don't know how long his judgment will last — but I do know he'll keep his people throughout the crisis, even if we have to face a great measure of suffering. And even in the most difficult times, we'll enjoy a time of great rejoicing — because he will reveal himself to us as never before.

God is going to keep his people in the coming crash!